God-Alone

D0050326

God Alone

HEARTFELT ENCOURAGEMENT FROM THE PAGES OF OUR DAILY BREAD

JOANIE YODER

Discovery House Publishers

Books, music, and videos that feed the soul with the Word of God

Box 3566 Grand Rapids, MI 49501

Discovery House Publishers is affiliated with RBC Ministries, Grand Rapids, Michigan.

Discovery House books are distributed to the trade exclusively by Barbour Publishing, Inc., Uhrichsville, Ohio.

Requests for permission to quote from this book should be directed to Permissions Department, Discovery House Publishers, P.O. Box 3566, Grand Rapids, MI 49501.

All scripture quotations, unless otherwise noted, are taken from the *Holy Bible, New International Version,* ®. *NIV*®. Copyright © 1973, 1978, 1984 by International Bible Society. Used by permission of Zondervan. All rights reserved.

Design and typesetting by Lakeside Design Plus

Library of Congress Cataloging-in-Publication Data

Yoder, Joanie, 1934–2004
    God alone : heartfelt encouragement from the pages of Our daily bread / Joanie Yoder.
        p. cm.
    ISBN 1-57293-201-5
    1. Meditations. I. Our daily bread. II. Title.
    BV4832.3.Y63 2006
    242—dc22

                                                    2006018794

Printed in the United States of America
06 07 08 09 10 11 / / 10 9 8 7 6 5 4 3 2 1

CONTENTS

Publisher's Foreword

A familiar name to *Our Daily Bread* readers, Joanie Yoder developed a faithful following as she connected with her audience in authentic, heartfelt devotionals. She wrote honestly of her life struggles and of her deep faith in the power of God alone to bring strength, comfort, and peace sufficient to meet the challenges of daily life.

In *God Alone*, we are privileged to provide a collection of Joanie's devotionals, which she began writing for *Our Daily Bread* in 1994. It is our hope that both those who are familiar with her writing as well as new readers will be encouraged through Joanie's stories of God's grace, His healing, and His unfailing sufficiency.

Through her personal struggles, Joanie learned the painful lessons of coping with life's disappointments: miscarriages, depression, and an addiction to prescription drugs. By her

9

own testimony, however, Joanie learned that the remedy for these challenges was God-dependence—"something for which we were created," she explained.

In an interview for the RBC television program *Day of Discovery*, Joanie described the motivating force of her life:

> Dependence on God is the theme of my life. My story is about a woman who had nothing in herself but found everything she needed through a life of dependence on God. It's not a sad state of affairs to have to depend on God—it's God's perfect design. The creature becomes his or her very best when depending on the Creator. I used to depend on God as a last resort. Now it's the first thing I do!

Joanie conveyed this message clearly through her writing and speaking ministries, but its truth carried over into her life's work when she and her husband began working with drug addicts at a Christian rehabilitation center they founded in England.

Joanie continued to rely on God's strength when she lost her husband to cancer in 1982, and her *ODB* devotionals often focused on her struggles as a widow and God's faithful provision of comfort and peace. She herself died in 2004.

Joanie's desire was that others would come to an understanding that in order to have a fulfilling relationship with God, we need to "come to the place where there's nothing of us and all of God." May Joanie's words and experiences, recorded in her devotionals, point you to God alone as your source of strength and hope.

I am the true vine, and my Father is the gardener. He cuts off every branch in me that bears no fruit, while every branch that does bear fruit he prunes so that it will be even more fruitful. You are already clean because of the word I have spoken to you. <u>Remain in me, and I will remain in you.</u> No branch can bear fruit by itself; it must remain in the vine. Neither can you bear fruit unless you remain in me.

I am the vine; you are the branches. If a man remains in me and I in him, he <u>will</u> bear much fruit; apart from me you can do nothing. If anyone does not remain in me, he is like a branch that is thrown away and withers; such branches are picked up, thrown into the fire and burned. <u>If you remain in me and my words remain in you</u>, ask whatever you wish, and it will be given you. This is to my Father's glory, that you bear much fruit, showing yourselves to be my disciples.

As the Father has loved me, so have I loved you. Now remain in my love. <u>If you obey my commands, you will remain in my love</u>, just as I have obeyed my Father's commands and remain in his love. I have told you this so that <u>my joy may be in you and that your joy may be complete.</u>

JOHN 15:1–11

*S*everal years have passed since the publication of my book *Finding the God-Dependent Life*. It's the story of how I learned to depend on God through the gradual breakdown of my self-sufficiency. My inadequacies forced me to depend on Him. In time, it became clear that the same principles that helped me in a crisis could surely help me all the time. So God-dependence became my chosen way of life. The result was greater wholeness and fruitfulness.

A churchgoer who read my book commented to a friend, "If you ask me, Joanie Yoder depends on God too much!" To help me explain the God-dependent life, I've turned that comment into a question: Is it possible to depend on God too much?

Let's answer that question by asking another: Is it possible for a branch to depend too much on the vine? Catherine Marshall wrote, "The point is not that the branches will do better when they are attached to the vine. Unless attached, the branches must wither and die." Jesus taught that unless the branches (you and I) abide in the vine (remain dependent on Him), it's impossible for us to bear His fruit.

Is it possible to depend on God too much? Not if we are to be fruitful branches. What kind of branch are you?

~~~

FRUITFULNESS FOR CHRIST DEPENDS
ON FELLOWSHIP WITH CHRIST.

The LORD upholds all those who fall
*   and lifts up all who are bowed down.*
The eyes of all look to you,
*   and you give them their food at the proper time.*
You open your hand
*   and satisfy the desires of every living thing.*

The LORD is righteous in all his ways
*   and loving toward all he has made.*
The LORD is near to all who call on him,
*   to all who call on him in truth.*
He fulfills the desires of those who fear him;
*   he hears their cry and saves them.*
The LORD watches over all who love him,
*   but all the wicked he will destroy.*

My mouth will speak in praise of the LORD.
*   Let every creature praise his holy name*
*   for ever and ever.*

PSALM 145:14–21

One morning while shopping, I began chatting with a woman who was a radiant Christian. After mentioning that her income was extremely meager, she encouraged me when she shared this incident: "Recently our pastor asked if I needed special prayer for any material needs. I answered, 'Just pray that I'll know more of Christ, because through Him I receive all things!'" This woman obviously was in the habit of looking expectantly to God, the true supplier of her needs.

David began Psalm 145 with an eloquent burst of praise to God in the first thirteen verses. Then he wrote about our deep human needs and how those needs are satisfied by God's abundant and freely given supply (vv. 14–21).

What is it, then, that keeps this law of supply and demand from operating as God intended? The problem is that we often live as though we are self-sufficient. We're shocked when life reminds us that we aren't. But that's the revelation we need if we are to become God-dependent people. We must recognize that it is God alone who provides for our needs.

The Lord desires to be responsible for you and your needs today. Will you let Him?

~~~

OUR NEEDS CANNOT EXHAUST GOD'S SUPPLY.

Do good to your servant
     according to your word, O LORD.
Teach me knowledge and good judgment,
     for I believe in your commands.
Before I was afflicted I went astray,
     but now I obey your word.
You are good, and what you do is good;
     teach me your decrees.
Though the arrogant have smeared me with lies,
     I keep your precepts with all my heart.
Their hearts are callous and unfeeling,
     but I delight in your law.
It was good for me to be afflicted
     so that I might learn your decrees.
The law from your mouth is more precious to me
     than thousands of pieces of silver and gold.

PSALM 119:65–72

I was in my early thirties, a dedicated wife and mother, a Christian worker at my husband's side. Yet inwardly I found myself on a trip nobody wants to take—the trip downward. I was heading for that certain sort of breakdown that most of us resist, the breakdown of my stubborn self-sufficiency.

Finally I experienced the odd relief of hitting rock bottom, where I made an unexpected discovery: The rock on which I had been thrown was none other than Christ Himself. Cast on Him alone, I was in a position to rebuild the rest of my life, this time as a God-dependent person rather than the self-dependent person I had been. My rock-bottom experience became a turning point and one of the most vital spiritual developments of my life.

Most people feel anything but spiritual when they hit bottom. Their misery is often reinforced by Christians who take a very shortsighted view of what the sufferer is going through and why. But our heavenly Father is well pleased with what He intends to bring out of such a painful process. A person who knows the secret of the God-dependent life can say, "It was good for me to be afflicted so that I might learn your decrees" (Psalm 119:71).

WHEN CHRISTIANS HIT ROCK BOTTOM,
THEY FIND THAT CHRIST IS A FIRM FOUNDATION.

AMEN.

Now on his way to Jerusalem, Jesus traveled along the border between Samaria and Galilee. As he was going into a village, ten men who had leprosy met him. They stood at a distance and called out in a loud voice, "Jesus, Master, have pity on us!"

When he saw them, he said, "Go, show yourselves to the priests." And as they went, they were cleansed.

One of them, when he saw he was healed, came back, praising God in a loud voice. He threw himself at Jesus' feet and thanked him—and he was a Samaritan.

Jesus asked, "Were not all ten cleansed? Where are the other nine? Was no one found to return and give praise to God except this foreigner?" Then he said to him, "Rise and go; your faith has made you well."

LUKE 17:11–19

What of the 9?
Were they not made well?
Were they cleansed, only to
have the leprosy return?

18

A few years ago, an unkempt, poorly adjusted youth named Tim (not his real name) was converted to Christ in an evangelistic crusade. A few days later, still unkempt but bathed in the love of Christ, he was sent to my home so that I could help him find a good church. And so it was that he began attending mine.

Though Tim needed and received much loving help in personal grooming and basic social graces, one characteristic has remained unchanged—his untamed love for his Savior.

One Sunday after church Tim rushed to my side, looking somewhat perplexed. He lamented, "Why me? I keep asking myself, why me?" Oh, no, I thought, he's become another complaining Christian. Then with arms outstretched, he went on to say, "Out of all the people in the world who are greater and smarter than I am, why did God choose me?" With that he joyfully clapped his hands.

Over the years I've heard many Christians, including myself, ask "Why me?" during tough times. But Tim is the first one I've heard ask that question when talking about God's blessings. Many were converted the same night as Tim, but I wonder how many among them have humbly asked, "Why me?" May we ask it often.

GRATITUDE SHOULD BE A CONTINUOUS ATTITUDE, NOT AN OCCASIONAL INCIDENT.

Lord, help me to show You my gratitude for all You've done for me on a continual basis. ♡

I will send my terror ahead of you and throw into confusion every nation you encounter. I will make all your enemies turn their backs and run. I will send the hornet ahead of you to drive the Hivites, Canaanites and Hittites out of your way. But I will not drive them out in a single year, because the land would become desolate and the wild animals too numerous for you. Little by little I will drive them out before you, until you have increased enough to take possession of the land.

EXODUS 23:27-30

Little by little... 7/30/07
Lord, is that how You plan
to heal me? I'm waiting.

20

When I was a little girl, my mother gave me her prized "reader" to help me learn, just as it had helped her years earlier. I loved one particular story, never dreaming how much it would affect me years later.

It was about a little boy with a small shovel. He was trying to clear a pathway through deep, new-fallen snow in front of his house. A man paused to observe the child's enormous task. "Little boy," he inquired, "how can someone as small as you expect to finish a task as big as this?" The boy looked up and replied confidently, "Little by little, that's how!" And he continued shoveling.

God awakened the seed of that story at a time when I was recovering from a breakdown. I remember how my "adult" self taunted the weak "child" within me: "How can someone as inadequate as you expect to surmount so great a mountain as this?" That little boy's reply became my reply: "Little by little, that's how!" And I did overcome—by depending on God. But it was one small victory after another.

The obstacles facing Israel as they considered claiming the land God had promised them must have seemed insurmountable. But He didn't ask them to do it all at once.

"LITTLE BY LITTLE" IS AN EFFECTIVE STRATEGY FOR VICTORY. TRUST GOD TO MOVE YOUR MOUNTAIN, BUT KEEP ON DIGGING.

And we know that in all things God works for the good of those who love him, who have been called according to his purpose. For those God foreknew he also predestined to be conformed to the likeness of his Son, that he might be the firstborn among many brothers. And those he predestined, he also called; those he called, he also justified; those he justified, he also glorified . . .

For I am convinced that neither death nor life, neither angels nor demons, neither the present nor the future, nor any powers, neither height nor depth, nor anything else in all creation, will be able to separate us from the love of God that is in Christ Jesus our Lord.

ROMANS 8:28–30, 38–39

Romans 8:28—how easily and how often this Bible reference rolls off our tongues! But perhaps we need to grasp more fully what this verse is really saying.

Randy Alcorn, in a book he co-authored with his wife, Nanci, offers some insights on Romans 8:28. He quotes the New American Standard Bible translation of this verse: "God causes all things to work together for good." Randy points out that it doesn't say each individual thing is good, but that God works them together for good.

Recalling his boyhood days, Randy tells how he often watched his mother bake cakes. One day when she had all the ingredients set out—flour, sugar, baking powder, raw egg, vanilla—he sneaked a taste of each one. Except for the sugar, they all tasted horrible. Then his mother stirred them together and put the batter in the oven. "It didn't make sense to me," he recalls, "that the combination of individually distasteful things produced such a tasty product."

Randy concludes that God likewise "takes all the undesirable stresses in our lives, mixes them together, puts them under the heat of crisis, and produces a perfect result."

Let's look beyond our immediate circumstances and remember that God has an ultimate good purpose.

WHEN THINGS LOOK BAD, DON'T FORGET:
GOD IS GOOD

Therefore, since we are surrounded by such a great cloud of witnesses, let us throw off everything that hinders and the sin that so easily entangles, and let us run with perseverance the race marked out for us . . .

In your struggle against sin, you have not yet resisted to the point of shedding your blood. And you have forgotten that word of encouragement that addresses you as sons:

> *"My son, do not make light of the Lord's discipline,*
> *and do not lose heart when he rebukes you,*
> *because the Lord disciplines those he loves, and he punishes*
> *everyone he accepts as a son."*

Endure hardship as discipline; God is treating you as sons. For what son is not disciplined by his father? . . . No discipline seems pleasant at the time, but painful. Later on, however, it produces a harvest of righteousness and peace for those who have been trained by it.

HEBREWS 12:1, 4–7, 11

I was in my second year of widowhood, and I was struggling. Morning after morning my prayer life consisted of one daily sigh: "Lord, I shouldn't be struggling like this!"

"And why not?" His still, small voice asked me from within one morning.

Then the answer came—unrecognized pride! Somehow I had thought that a person of my spiritual maturity should be beyond such struggle. What a ridiculous thought, since I had never been a widow before and needed the freedom to be a true learner, even a struggling learner.

At the same time, I was reminded of the story of a man who took home a cocoon so he could watch the emperor moth emerge. As the moth struggled to get through the tiny opening, the man enlarged it with the snip of his scissors. The moth emerged easily—but its wings were shriveled. The struggle through the narrow opening is God's way to force fluid from its body into its wings. The "merciful" snip, in reality, was cruel.

Hebrews 12 describes the Christian life as an effort that involves discipline, correction, and training in righteousness. Surely such a race could not be run without a holy striving against self and sin. Sometimes the struggle is exactly what we need.

~~

GOD'S CHASTENING IS COMPASSIONATE, NEVER CRUEL.

Then Jesus said to the crowds and to his disciples: "The teachers of the law and the Pharisees sit in Moses' seat. So you must obey them and do everything they tell you. But do not do what they do, for they do not practice what they preach. They tie up heavy loads and put them on men's shoulders, but they themselves are not willing to lift a finger to move them.

"Everything they do is done for men to see: They make their phylacteries wide and the tassels on their garments long; they love the place of honor at banquets and the most important seats in the synagogues; they love to be greeted in the marketplaces and to have men call them 'Rabbi' . . .

"The greatest among you will be your servant. For whoever exalts himself will be humbled, and whoever humbles himself will be exalted."

MATTHEW 23:1–7, 11–12

*S*ome opponents of Christianity may not be so much against Christ as they are against hypocrisy. Ironically, it hasn't occurred to them that no one was more opposed to hypocrisy than Christ Himself.

We've all met scoffers who mindlessly parrot the phrase, "The church is full of hypocrites!" But let's not be mindless in our response and dismiss such pronouncements without taking heed lest they be true.

We tend to think that it's not true of us. But let's think again. How many times have we been like the Christian woman who glanced through her window, only to see a nosy, noisy neighbor approaching her door! Her young, impressionable children heard her as she growled, "Oh, no— not her again!" Whereupon she opened the door and gushed insincerely, "How very nice to see you!"

Our lips and our lives often preach a mixed message. In Matthew 23, Jesus described the hypocritical teachers of the law and warned His disciples, "Do not do what they do, for they do not practice what they preach (v. 3).

God forbid that some opponent of Christ would be influenced by careless hypocrisy in our lives. Lord, help us to be careful "preachers."

~~~

HYPOCRITES PRAY ON THEIR KNEES ON SUNDAY
AND PREY ON THEIR NEIGHBORS ON MONDAY.

Everyone who believes that Jesus is the Christ is born of God, and everyone who loves the father loves his child as well. This is how we know that we love the children of God: by loving God and carrying out his commands. This is love for God: to obey his commands. And his commands are not burdensome, for everyone born of God overcomes the world. This is the victory that has overcome the world, even our faith. Who is it that overcomes the world? Only he who believes that Jesus is the Son of God . . .

And this is the testimony: God has given us eternal life, and this life is in his Son. He who has the Son has life; he who does not have the Son of God does not have life.

I write these things to you who believe in the name of the Son of God so that you may know that you have eternal life.

1 JOHN 5:1–5, 11–13

Sadly, many true Christians are plagued with doubt about their salvation. Even though they have come in repentance and faith to Jesus as their Savior, they still wonder, "Am I really saved?"

My late husband, Bill, often told about something that happened to him when he was two years old. One day he disobediently strayed from home and got lost. When his parents realized that he was missing, they went out searching for him. Finally, to everyone's immense relief, they spotted their tearful boy and carried him safely home.

Days later, Billy overheard his mother relate this incident to a visitor. When she reached the part where they went out searching for him, Billy began to relive the story. "Mommy, Mommy!" he sobbed. "Did you ever find me?" Surprised and deeply touched by his doubt, she embraced him and said, "Of course, my child! Don't you remember that happy moment? See, you're with us now, and we'll make sure that you always are." That settled it for Billy. He simply believed her word.

The New Testament letter of 1 John was written to give believers the assurance of salvation. That assurance can be yours as you take God at His word.

~~~

CHRIST'S WORK MAKES US SAFE;
GOD'S WORD MAKES US SURE.

The vision of Obadiah.

This is what the Sovereign LORD says about Edom—
   We have heard a message from the LORD:
   An envoy was sent to the nations to say,
      "Rise, and let us go against her for battle"—
"See, I will make you small among the nations;
   you will be utterly despised.
The pride of your heart has deceived you,
   you who live in the clefts of the rocks
   and make your home on the heights,
   you who say to yourself,
      'Who can bring me down to the ground?'
Though you soar like the eagle
   and make your nest among the stars,
   from there I will bring you down,"
   declares the LORD.

OBADIAH vv. 1–4

My daughter travels all over the world as a flight attendant and often comes home with some fascinating tales. One such story is about former heavyweight boxing champion Muhammad Ali, who was seated in an aircraft that was preparing for takeoff. A flight attendant, noticing that he did not have his seatbelt fastened, asked him kindly, "Excuse me, sir, but would you mind fastening your seatbelt?"

As the story goes, Muhammad Ali looked up with that saucy grin of his and said in a slow, gravelly voice, "Superman don't need no seatbelt!" Without missing a beat, the flight attendant packed a punch with this quick reply: "Superman don't need no airplane, so how about fastening up!"

Of course, Ali was only joking. If a person really believed he was Superman, he would be seriously deluded. He would be like the ancient Edomites in Obadiah who had been deceived by their own pride. The truth is, we all have the same tendency.

A. W. Tozer aptly described the kind of Christians the Lord longs for us to be: "Men and women who have stopped being 'fooled' about their own strength and are not afraid of being 'caught' depending on their all-sufficient Lord."

~~~

TO EXPERIENCE GOD'S STRENGTH,
WE MUST ADMIT OUR WEAKNESS.

Some of the elders of Israel came to me and sat down in front of me. Then the word of the LORD came to me: "Son of man, these men have set up idols in their hearts and put wicked stumbling blocks before their faces. Should I let them inquire of me at all? Therefore speak to them and tell them, 'This is what the Sovereign LORD says: When any Israelite sets up idols in his heart and puts a wicked stumbling block before his face and then goes to a prophet, I the LORD will answer him myself in keeping with his great idolatry. I will do this to recapture the hearts of the people of Israel, who have all deserted me for their idols.'

"Therefore say to the house of Israel, 'This is what the Sovereign LORD says: Repent! Turn from your idols and renounce all your detestable practices!

" 'When any Israelite or any alien living in Israel separates himself from me and sets up idols in his heart and puts a wicked stumbling block before his face and then goes to a prophet to inquire of me, I the LORD will answer him myself. I will set my face against that man and make him an example and a byword. I will cut him off from my people. Then you will know that I am the LORD.' "

EZEKIEL 14:1−8

When my husband and I first went out as missionaries, I recall being concerned about the growth of materialism in our society. It never crossed my mind that I myself could be materialistic. After all, hadn't we gone overseas with almost nothing? Didn't we have to live in a shabbily furnished, rundown apartment? I thought materialism couldn't touch us.

Nonetheless, feelings of discontent gradually began to take root in my heart. Before long I was craving nice things and secretly feeling resentful over not having them. Then one day God's Spirit opened my eyes with a disturbing insight: Materialism isn't necessarily having things; it can also be craving them. There I stood—guilty of materialism! God had exposed my discontentment for what it was—an idol in my heart! That day as I repented of this subtle sin, God recaptured my heart as His rightful throne. Needless to say, a deep contentment followed, based not on things but on Him.

In Ezekiel's day, God dealt thoroughly with this kind of secret idolatry. His throne on earth has always been in the hearts of His people. That's why we must rid our hearts of anything that destroys our contentment with Him.

~~~

AN IDOL IS ANYTHING THAT TAKES THE PLACE OF GOD.

Devote yourselves to prayer, being watchful and thankful. And pray for us, too, that God may open a door for our message, so that we may proclaim the mystery of Christ, for which I am in chains. Pray that I may proclaim it clearly, as I should. Be wise in the way you act toward outsiders; make the most of every opportunity. Let your conversation be always full of grace, seasoned with salt, so that you may know how to answer everyone.

COLOSSIANS 4:2-6

*W*ords of encouragement can be "life words," bringing new motivation to our lives. Mark Twain said that he could live for a whole month on one good compliment!

Christian encouragement, however, is more than a compliment or a pat on the back, valuable as these can be. One writer described it as "the kind of expression that helps someone want to be a better Christian, even when life is rough."

As a youth, Larry Crabb had developed a stutter that humiliated him in a school assembly. A short time later when praying aloud in a church service, his stutter caused him to get both his words and his theology mixed up in his prayer. Expecting stern correction, Larry slipped out of the service, resolving never to speak in public again. On his way out he was stopped by an older man who said, "Larry, there's one thing I want you to know. Whatever you do for the Lord, I'm behind you one thousand percent." Larry's resolve never again to speak publicly weakened instantly. Now, many years later, he addresses large crowds without stuttering.

Paul told us to season our speech "with salt" so that we may know how to answer others (Colossians 4:6). Then we will speak "life words" that bring encouragement.

~~~

CORRECTION MAY MOLD US,
BUT ENCOURAGEMENT WILL MOTIVATE US.

Then Jehoshaphat stood up in the assembly of Judah and Jerusalem at the temple of the Lord in the front of the new courtyard and said: . . .

"O our God, will you not judge them? For we have no power to face this vast army that is attacking us. We do not know what to do, but our eyes are upon you."

All the men of Judah, with their wives and children and little ones, stood there before the LORD.

Then the Spirit of the LORD came upon Jahaziel son of Zechariah, the son of Benaiah, the son of Jeiel, the son of Mattaniah, a Levite and descendant of Asaph, as he stood in the assembly.

He said: "Listen, King Jehoshaphat and all who live in Judah and Jerusalem! This is what the LORD says to you: 'Do not be afraid or discouraged because of this vast army. For the battle is not yours, but God's. Tomorrow march down against them. They will be climbing up by the Pass of Ziz, and you will find them at the end of the gorge in the Desert of Jeruel. You will not have to fight this battle. Take up your positions; stand firm and see the deliverance the LORD will give you, O Judah and Jerusalem. Do not be afraid; do not be discouraged. Go out to face them tomorrow, and the LORD will be with you.'"

2 CHRONICLES 20:5-6, 12-17

A wise Bible teacher once said, "Sooner or later God will bring self-sufficient people to the place where they have no resource but Him: no strength, no answers, nothing but Him. Without God's help, they're sunk."

He then told of a despairing man who confessed to his pastor, "My life is really in bad shape." "How bad?" the pastor inquired. Burying his head in his hands, he moaned, "I'll tell you how bad—all I've got left is God." The pastor's face lit up. "I'm happy to assure you that a person with nothing left but God has more than enough for great victory!"

In 2 Chronicles 20, the people of Judah were also in trouble. They admitted their lack of power and wisdom to conquer their foes. All they had left was God! But King Jehoshaphat and the people saw this as reason for hope, not despair. "Our eyes are upon you," they declared to God (2 Chronicles 20:12). And their hope was not disappointed as He fulfilled His promise: "The battle is not yours, but God's" (v.15).

Are you in a position where all self-sufficiency is gone? As you turn your eyes on the Lord and put your hope in Him, you have God's reassuring promise that you need nothing more.

~~~

WHEN GOD IS ALL YOU'VE GOT,
YOU'VE GOT MORE THAN ENOUGH.

The LORD is my shepherd, I shall not be in want.
He makes me lie down in green pastures,
he leads me beside quiet waters,
he restores my soul.
He guides me in paths of righteousness
for his name's sake.
Even though I walk
through the valley of the shadow of death,
I will fear no evil,
for you are with me;
your rod and your staff,
they comfort me.

You prepare a table before me
in the presence of my enemies.
You anoint my head with oil;
my cup overflows.
Surely goodness and love will follow me
all the days of my life,
and I will dwell in the house of the LORD
forever.

PSALM 23

*I*n her down-to-earth book *More Than Sparrows*, Mary Welch tells of her discussion with a group of high schoolers about worry. Although they were Christians, they were as worried as pagans about the common things of life. As she listened to them with love, yearning to help them, an unusual idea came to her for a game they could play. It went like this: Instead of saying, "I'm worried," stop and say, "The Lord is my Shepherd." Then add, "So I'm worried to death!" The students laughed at the idea, but they all promised to play this new "peace-of-mind" game.

Later Mary received a phone call from a young woman who had been paralyzed by worry over an exam she had been dreading to take. She said, "I must tell you how the game helped me trust God today. As I froze with worry, I remembered to say, 'The Lord is my Shepherd . . . so I'm afraid I'll fail!' Suddenly I felt the strangest peace of mind. I laughed at myself, then I took the exam and passed!"

Saying in one breath, "The Lord is my Shepherd, and I am worried to death" is more than a mind game to point out the absurdity of worry. God can use it to bring us to a fuller trust in Him.

~~~

WORRY IS THE INTEREST YOU PAY
ON BORROWED TROUBLE.

Before the years of famine came, two sons were born to Joseph by Asenath daughter of Potiphera, priest of On. Joseph named his firstborn Manasseh and said, "It is because God has made me forget all my trouble and all my father's household." The second son he named Ephraim and said, "It is because God has made me fruitful in the land of my suffering."

The seven years of abundance in Egypt came to an end, and the seven years of famine began, just as Joseph had said. There was famine in all the other lands, but in the whole land of Egypt there was food. When all Egypt began to feel the famine, the people cried to Pharaoh for food. Then Pharaoh told all the Egyptians, "Go to Joseph and do what he tells you."

When the famine had spread over the whole country, Joseph opened the storehouses and sold grain to the Egyptians, for the famine was severe throughout Egypt. And all the countries came to Egypt to buy grain from Joseph, because the famine was severe in all the world.

GENESIS 41:50–57

*W*hen seemingly needless suffering invades our lives, we often ask ourselves, "Who needs all this grief?" But consider, for a moment, the origin of pearls.

Each pearl is formed by an oyster's internal response to a wound caused by an irritant, such as a grain of sand. Resources of repair rush to the injured area. The final result is a lustrous pearl. Something beautiful is created that would have been impossible without the wound.

In Genesis 41, we see Joseph in a position of influence, a position God soon used to feed surrounding nations and Joseph's family during famine. But how did he become influential? It began with a wound—being sold into slavery (Genesis 37)—which produced a pearl of usefulness. Because Joseph drew on God's resources when humiliated, he became better, not bitter. He named his second son Ephraim, which means "twice fruitful," and he said, "God has made me fruitful in the land of my suffering" (Genesis 41:52).

Author Paul E. Billheimer says of Joseph, "If human pity could have rescued him from the sad part of his life, the glorious part that followed would have been lost." So if you're suffering, remember: No wounds, no pearls!

~~~

ADVERSITIES ARE OFTEN BLESSINGS IN DISGUISE.

People were bringing little children to Jesus to have him touch them, but the disciples rebuked them. When Jesus saw this, he was indignant. He said to them, "Let the little children come to me, and do not hinder them, for the kingdom of God belongs to such as these. I tell you the truth, anyone who will not receive the kingdom of God like a little child will never enter it." And he took the children in his arms, put his hands on them and blessed them.

MARK 10:13-16

While Jesus lived on this earth, He took little children in His arms and blessed them (Mark 10:16). And He is still in the child-embracing ministry today.

My friend told me about a touching conversation between her two grandchildren. Five-year-old Matthew said to Sarah, age three, "I talk to Jesus in my head!" She responded, "I don't—I just cuddle with Him!"

Many other children of God, much older ones, have experienced His unseen everlasting arms around them and beneath them. Brother Lawrence, the seventeenth-century monk known for sensing the presence of God amid the pots and pans of the monastery's kitchen, spoke of being "known of God and extremely caressed by Him." And Hudson Taylor, the pioneer missionary to China, scrawled this note as he neared the end of his life: "I am so weak that I cannot work; I cannot read my Bible; I cannot even pray. I can only lie still in God's arms like a child, and trust."

God wants us to nestle close to Him in childlike trust, whether young or old, strong or weak. In response, through His indwelling Spirit, He draws us to Himself to comfort and to bless. Have you and God had a hug of the heart today?

DON'T WRESTLE—JUST NESTLE. —CORRIE TEN BOOM

So [Jesus] came to a town in Samaria called Sychar, near the plot of ground Jacob had given to his son Joseph. Jacob's well was there, and Jesus, tired as he was from the journey, sat down by the well. It was about the sixth hour.

When a Samaritan woman came to draw water, Jesus said to her, "Will you give me a drink?" (His disciples had gone into the town to buy food.)

The Samaritan woman said to him, "You are a Jew and I am a Samaritan woman. How can you ask me for a drink?" (For Jews do not associate with Samaritans.)

Jesus answered her, "If you knew the gift of God and who it is that asks you for a drink, you would have asked him and he would have given you living water."

"Sir," the woman said, "you have nothing to draw with and the well is deep. Where can you get this living water? Are you greater than our father Jacob, who gave us the well and drank from it himself, as did also his sons and his flocks and herds?"

Jesus answered, "Everyone who drinks this water will be thirsty again, but whoever drinks the water I give him will never thirst. Indeed, the water I give him will become in him a spring of water welling up to eternal life."

The woman said to him, "Sir, give me this water so that I won't get thirsty and have to keep coming here to draw water."

JOHN 4:5–15

*I*n John 4, we see Jesus weary, hungry, and thirsty. He was just as human as we are. He was also God and could have met all His own needs. But Jesus didn't insist on doing everything without the help of others. On this occasion He graciously (and no doubt gratefully) allowed His disciples to go and buy food while He sat by the well to rest and wait. And when a Samaritan woman of questionable character came to draw water, He did what many of us might hesitate to do—He asked her for a drink.

For years I missed an important lesson in our Lord's vulnerability, until He taught me, through a friend, the subtle selfishness of not letting others help us. One day this friend tried to do a kindness for me, and as usual I resisted. In frustration she said, "You know what? You're an ungenerous receiver!"

Instantly I saw it! Quite rightly, I had always tried to live by Jesus' words, "It is more blessed to give than to receive" (Acts 20:35). The trouble was, in the name of being unselfish, I always had to be the giver.

Others desire to experience the blessedness of giving, but we often frustrate their giving by refusing their help. Let's learn to be generous receivers—just like Jesus.

~

BE AS GRACIOUS IN RECEIVING AS YOU ARE IN GIVING.

The length of our days is seventy years—
*   or eighty, if we have the strength;*
yet their span is but trouble and sorrow,
*   for they quickly pass, and we fly away.*

Who knows the power of your anger?
*   For your wrath is as great as the fear that is due you.*
Teach us to number our days aright,
*   that we may gain a heart of wisdom.*

Relent, O Lord! How long will it be?
*   Have compassion on your servants.*
Satisfy us in the morning with your unfailing love,
*   that we may sing for joy and be glad all our days.*
Make us glad for as many days as you have afflicted us,
*   for as many years as we have seen trouble.*

PSALM 90:10–15

We call life's older years the "sunset years." But are they really that rosy? For some, they are. But for many others, even Christians, the sunset years may become clouded with bitterness or despair.

To minimize this, we must make it our goal early in life to get the right focus. Robert Kastenbaum understood this. He wrote, "I do feel an increased sense of responsibility to this future self and to all those who cross my path. What kind of old man will I be, given the chance? The answer to that question depends largely on the kind of person I am right now."

As I have observed contented older people, I've learned that it is our focus more than our feelings that determines the sort of people we are. I once visited a godly woman in her nineties who was feeling her age in every joint and organ. "Old age ain't for sissies!" she groaned honestly. Then, as always, her groans gave way to praise for God's goodness. A focus of gratitude, begun early in life, parted the clouds and let the sun shine through.

What is your focus today, regardless of your feelings? Is it one of gratitude for Jesus and His gift of eternal life? If so, you'll grow sweeter as you grow older.

~~

WHAT YOU WILL BE TOMORROW DEPENDS
ON THE CHOICES YOU MAKE TODAY.

I tell you the truth, the man who does not enter the sheep pen by the gate, but climbs in by some other way, is a thief and a robber. The man who enters by the gate is the shepherd of his sheep. The watchman opens the gate for him, and the sheep listen to his voice. He calls his own sheep by name and leads them out. When he has brought out all his own, he goes on ahead of them, and his sheep follow him because they know his voice. But they will never follow a stranger; in fact, they will run away from him because they do not recognize a stranger's voice . . .

I am the good shepherd. The good shepherd lays down his life for the sheep.

JOHN 10:1–5, 11

A few years ago, I was invited to speak on the subject of guidance. In my preparation, I opened my concordance to look up the word *guidance*, expecting to find a long list of verses promising guidance from God. To my surprise, *guidance* wasn't there. Instead, I found the word *guide* and a number of verses promising that God Himself would be the guide of His people.

This discovery added fresh insight to my Christian pilgrimage. I was reminded that people who are blind need guide dogs, not guidance dogs! Even if dogs were capable of talking, how unsatisfactory it would be if they were mere bystanders, shouting warnings to the blind from a distance: "Careful now! You're approaching a hole. Watch out for the curb!" No, these mute but faithful creatures escort their sightless companions every step of the way, being their eyes, and steering them safely along precarious pathways.

Some people want God to be like a glorified advice bureau. But when our sight is dim and our way is dark, as it often is, we need more than good advice—we need the Good Shepherd to lead us (John 10:3, 11).

As we follow Christ each day, we'll have all the guidance we'll ever need.

~~~

IF YOU'RE LOOKING FOR GUIDANCE,
FOLLOW CHRIST YOUR GUIDE.

Now I rejoice in what was suffered for you, and I fill up in my flesh what is still lacking in regard to Christ's afflictions, for the sake of his body, which is the church. I have become its servant by the commission God gave me to present to you the word of God in its fullness—the mystery that has been kept hidden for ages and generations, but is now disclosed to the saints. To them God has chosen to make known among the Gentiles the glorious riches of this mystery, which is Christ in you, the hope of glory. We proclaim him, admonishing and teaching everyone with all wisdom, so that we may present everyone perfect in Christ. To this end I labor, struggling with all his energy, which so powerfully works in me.

COLOSSIANS 1:24–29

When John became a salesman in a well-known insurance company years ago, his aim was to work effectively in his firm without compromising his Christian integrity. But there were those who considered him naive. In their view, one could possess job security or Christian integrity—not both.

But John did not waver in his commitment to be a godly witness in the business world. Although he was in a job that required accurate calculations, he had a weakness when it came to simple arithmetic. This forced him to depend more on Christ in everything, which enhanced his witness.

John eventually became the company's top salesman, and God used him to win many colleagues to Christ. Later, as branch manager, John and his team became the company's largest branch worldwide—all without compromising Christian integrity.

Are you striving to live and work without compromise in a tough place? Are you doing your best, but your best is not enough? Colossians 1:29 reminds us that dependence on God's mighty power within us is what makes us effective. John, the businessman, summed it up like this: "God helps me do better than I can!"

He will do the same for you.

~

MAY OUR BOAST BE NOT IN WHAT WE DO FOR CHRIST,
BUT IN WHAT CHRIST DOES FOR US.

After [Paul and Silas] had been severely flogged, they were thrown into prison, and the jailer was commanded to guard them carefully. Upon receiving such orders, he put them in the inner cell and fastened their feet in the stocks.

About midnight Paul and Silas were praying and singing hymns to God, and the other prisoners were listening to them. Suddenly there was such a violent earthquake that the foundations of the prison were shaken. At once all the prison doors flew open, and everybody's chains came loose. The jailer woke up, and when he saw the prison doors open, he drew his sword and was about to kill himself because he thought the prisoners had escaped. But Paul shouted, "Don't harm yourself! We are all here!"

The jailer called for lights, rushed in and fell trembling before Paul and Silas. He then brought them out and asked, "Sirs, what must I do to be saved?"

They replied, "Believe in the Lord Jesus, and you will be saved— you and your household." Then they spoke the word of the Lord to him and to all the others in his house. At that hour of the night the jailer took them and washed their wounds; then immediately he and all his family were baptized. The jailer brought them into his house and set a meal before them; he was filled with joy because he had come to believe in God—he and his whole family.

ACTS 16:23–34

*F*inding the right questions is as crucial as finding the right answers," says devotional writer Henri Nouwen. Yet how easy it is to run ahead of God's Spirit as we talk to nonbelievers about Christ, giving prepackaged answers before we listen to their questions.

This tendency was highlighted several years ago when someone scrawled the words "Christ is the answer!" on the side of a building. A cynical passerby added these words: "What is the question?"

Paul and Silas, thrown into prison for the gospel's sake, provoked a deep spiritual question in the heart of their jailer. This wasn't achieved, however, by preaching a three-point sermon at him. Instead, they prayed and sang hymns to God. When an earthquake opened the prison doors and broke their chains, the jailer tried to kill himself, fearing that he would be put to death if his prisoners escaped. But Paul and Silas stopped him by choosing to stay in prison for his sake. At this he cried out, "Sirs, what must I do to be saved?" (Acts 16:30).

Today, as then, the Spirit will create the right questions in people's hearts and make them ready for the right answer—Jesus Christ.

CHRISTIANS WORTH THEIR SALT
MAKE OTHERS THIRSTY FOR THE WATER OF LIFE.

He made known his ways to Moses,
  his deeds to the people of Israel:
The LORD is compassionate and gracious,
  slow to anger, abounding in love.
He will not always accuse,
  nor will he harbor his anger forever;
he does not treat us as our sins deserve
  or repay us according to our iniquities.
For as high as the heavens are above the earth,
  so great is his love for those who fear him;
as far as the east is from the west,
  so far has he removed our transgressions from us.
As a father has compassion on his children,
  so the LORD has compassion on those who fear him;
for he knows how we are formed,
  he remembers that we are dust.

PSALM 103:7–14

ost Christians would prefer to see God perform mighty miracles rather than to have fellowship with Him and learn His ways.

Today's text says that God made known His mighty acts to the people of Israel, but to Moses He "made known His ways." Exodus 33 records a great crisis in which Moses humbly prayed, "If you are pleased with me, teach me your ways" (v. 13). He wanted to know God and His plans for His people more than to see another mighty miracle. No wonder the Lord conversed with him "as a man speaks with his friend" (v. 11).

Commenting on the difference between ways and acts, F. B. Meyer wrote, "Ways, or plans, are only made known to the inner circle of the saints; the ordinary congregation learns only His acts."

A talented friend of mine, Jennifer, learned this difference after spending several years in a wheelchair. One day she tearfully prayed, "Lord, I could have done so much for You, if only I could have been healthy." God's response was inaudible but clear: "Many people work for Me, but very few are willing to be My friend."

If you desire to know God personally more than you long to see His mighty miracles, you'll be satisfied.

~~~

KNOWING GOD IS NOT ONLY SEEING HIS WORKS
BUT ALSO LEARNING HIS WAYS.

Yes, and I will continue to rejoice, for I know that through your prayers and the help given by the Spirit of Jesus Christ, what has happened to me will turn out for my deliverance. I eagerly expect and hope that I will in no way be ashamed, but will have sufficient courage so that now as always Christ will be exalted in my body, whether by life or by death. For to me, to live is Christ and to die is gain. If I am to go on living in the body, this will mean fruitful labor for me. Yet what shall I choose? I do not know! I am torn between the two: I desire to depart and be with Christ, which is better by far; but it is more necessary for you that I remain in the body. Convinced of this, I know that I will remain, and I will continue with all of you for your progress and joy in the faith, so that through my being with you again your joy in Christ Jesus will overflow on account of me.

PHILIPPIANS 1:18–26

*L*ois had just undergone cancer surgery and was alone with her thoughts. She had faced death before, or so she thought, but it had always been the death of people she had loved—not her own.

Suddenly she realized that losing someone she loved was more threatening to her than the possibility of losing her own life. She wondered why. She remembered what she had asked herself before her operation, "Am I ready to die?" Her immediate answer had been and still was, "Yes, I am. Christ is my Lord and Savior."

With her readiness for death secure, she now needed to concentrate on living. Would it be in fear or in faith? Then God seemed to say, "I have saved you from eternal death. I want to save you from living in fear." Isaiah 43:1 came to mind: "I have redeemed you; I have summoned you by name; you are mine."

Now Lois testifies, "Yes, I am His! That's the reality that is more important than doctors telling me I have cancer." And then she adds, "I win either way!"

Lois's insight is a convinced echo of Paul's words in Philippians 1:21: "For to me, to live is Christ and to die is gain." Let's pray that those words may resonate in our hearts. That confidence makes us winners either way.

~~

WE CAN REALLY LIVE WHEN WE'RE READY TO DIE.

They came back to Moses and Aaron and the whole Israelite community at Kadesh in the Desert of Paran. There they reported to them and to the whole assembly and showed them the fruit of the land. They gave Moses this account: "We went into the land to which you sent us, and it does flow with milk and honey! Here is its fruit. But the people who live there are powerful, and the cities are fortified and very large. We even saw descendants of Anak there. The Amalekites live in the Negev; the Hittites, Jebusites and Amorites live in the hill country; and the Canaanites live near the sea and along the Jordan."

Then Caleb silenced the people before Moses and said, "We should go up and take possession of the land, for we can certainly do it."

But the men who had gone up with him said, "We can't attack those people; they are stronger than we are." And they spread among the Israelites a bad report about the land they had explored. They said, "The land we explored devours those living in it. All the people we saw there are of great size. We saw the Nephilim there (the descendants of Anak come from the Nephilim). We seemed like grasshoppers in our own eyes, and we looked the same to them."

NUMBERS 13:26–33

*L*ike the children of Israel in Numbers 13, Hannah Hurnard, author of *Hinds' Feet on High Places*, was once paralyzed by fear. Then she heard a sermon on scarecrows that challenged her to turn her fear into faith.

The preacher said, "A wise bird knows that a scarecrow is simply an advertisement. It announces that some very juicy and delicious fruit is to be had for the picking. There are scarecrows in all the best gardens . . . If I am wise, I too shall treat the scarecrow as though it were an invitation. Every giant in the way which makes me feel like a grasshopper is only a scarecrow beckoning me to God's richest blessings." He concluded, "Faith is a bird which loves to perch on scarecrows. All our fears are groundless."

Hannah testified that this humble parable has encouraged her to walk along some frightening but fruitful pathways more times than she could number.

What is your scarecrow today? Difficult circumstances? Personal inadequacy? Uncertainty? The enemy of your soul wants to keep you away from the place of God's blessing. Perch on your scarecrow by faith, start singing, and expect an abundant feast!

~~

WHEN YOU FIX YOUR EYES ON GOD,
YOUR FEARS WILL VANISH.

We know that the one who raised the Lord Jesus from the dead will also raise us with Jesus and present us with you in his presence. All this is for your benefit, so that the grace that is reaching more and more people may cause thanksgiving to overflow to the glory of God.

Therefore we do not lose heart. Though outwardly we are wasting away, yet inwardly we are being renewed day by day. For our light and momentary troubles are achieving for us an eternal glory that far outweighs them all. So we fix our eyes not on what is seen, but on what is unseen. For what is seen is temporary, but what is unseen is eternal.

Now we know that if the earthly tent we live in is destroyed, we have a building from God, an eternal house in heaven, not built by human hands.

2 CORINTHIANS 4:14–5:1

*W*ilfred Yoder is one of the most enthusiastic Christians I know, even though he has suffered with the pain of arthritis for many years. When people greet him and inquire, "How are you today?" he cheerfully answers, "Just fine!"

Those who know of his pain sometimes question his sincerity. "How can you say you're fine when you're in so much pain?" Wilfred's standard response is: "How I feel has very little to do with how I am. You see, the part of me that hurts is just a shell, not the real me, and the real me is just fine!"

What Wilfred calls a shell, Paul called a tent (2 Corinthians 5:1). And the apostle tells us that the "real me" that Wilfred refers to, the "inward Wilfred," is "being renewed day by day" (4:16).

Although Wilfred's earthly tent is painful and perishing, he realizes that it is after all just a temporary housing for the inward man. One day he will exchange it for his permanent home awaiting him in heaven. That is his confidence. But until then, the inward Wilfred is conscious of being renewed daily.

How are you today? Is your tent drooping? Remember, if Christ is your Savior and Lord, a perfect body awaits you one day. But until then, no matter what's on the outside, on the inside we can say, "I'm just fine!"

~~~

ALTHOUGH OUR BODY IS PERISHING,
OUR SPIRIT CAN BE FLOURISHING.

I consider that our present sufferings are not worth comparing with the glory that will be revealed in us. The creation waits in eager expectation for the sons of God to be revealed. For the creation was subjected to frustration, not by its own choice, but by the will of the one who subjected it, in hope that the creation itself will be liberated from its bondage to decay and brought into the glorious freedom of the children of God.

We know that the whole creation has been groaning as in the pains of childbirth right up to the present time. Not only so, but we ourselves, who have the firstfruits of the Spirit, groan inwardly as we wait eagerly for our adoption as sons, the redemption of our bodies. For in this hope we were saved. But hope that is seen is no hope at all. Who hopes for what he already has? But if we hope for what we do not yet have, we wait for it patiently.

In the same way, the Spirit helps us in our weakness. We do not know what we ought to pray for, but the Spirit himself intercedes for us with groans that words cannot express. And he who searches our hearts knows the mind of the Spirit, because the Spirit intercedes for the saints in accordance with God's will.

ROMANS 8:18–26

I once heard of a Christian seminar titled "How to Live a Stress-Free Life." Such an unrealistic hope promptly made me stressful! Yet we all long for relief.

A Christian friend of mine whose family is experiencing tough times admits feeling let down by God. She said, "I've prayed, agonized, and claimed promises, but nothing changes. The frustrating thing is that I know He has the power to get us out of this. I've seen Him do it before, but this time He's silent."

Larry Crabb, in his book *Inside Out*, emphasizes that our only hope for complete relief from hardship is to be with Jesus in heaven. "Until then," he says, "we either groan or pretend we don't." He adds, "The experience of groaning, however, is precisely what modern Christianity so often tries to help us escape."

My friend is groaning, and she's not pretending she isn't. Like all of us, she simply wants things to change. But the fact is, something is changing—she is! Paul assured us in 2 Corinthians 4:17 that our present sufferings are lightweight and brief compared with the weighty and eternal changes those sufferings are producing in us. So let's not lose heart. There's glory ahead! (Romans 8:18).

～

GOD OFTEN USES A SETBACK TO MOVE US AHEAD.

I will extol the LORD at all times;
  his praise will always be on my lips.
My soul will boast in the LORD;
  let the afflicted hear and rejoice.
Glorify the LORD with me;
  let us exalt his name together.
I sought the LORD, and he answered me;
  he delivered me from all my fears.
Those who look to him are radiant;
  their faces are never covered with shame.
This poor man called, and the LORD heard him;
  he saved him out of all his troubles.
The angel of the LORD encamps around those who fear him,
  and he delivers them.
Taste and see that the LORD is good;
  blessed is the man who takes refuge in him.

PSALM 34:1–8

*D*o you believe God is good, even when life isn't? Mary did, and I gasped with amazement the day I heard her pastor share her story at her funeral. She, being dead, yet speaks!

Mary had been a widow, very poor, and totally housebound because of her ailments in old age. But like the psalmist, she had learned to praise God amid her hardships. Over the years she had come to savor with deep gratitude every good thing He sent her way.

Her pastor said he occasionally would visit her at home. Because of her crippling pain, it took her a long time to inch her way to the door to let him in. So he would call on the telephone and tell her that he was on his way and when he would get there. Mary would then begin the slow, arduous journey to the door, reaching it about the time he arrived. Without fail, he could count on her greeting him with these triumphant words: "God is good!"

I've observed that those who speak most often about God's goodness are usually those with the most trials. They choose to focus on the Lord's mercy and grace rather than on their troubles, and in so doing they taste His goodness.

Mary not only challenges us to taste and see, but to taste and say that the Lord is good—even when life isn't.

THOSE WHO BLESS GOD IN THEIR TRIALS WILL
BE BLESSED BY GOD THROUGH THEIR TRIALS.

Since, then, you have been raised with Christ, set your hearts on things above, where Christ is seated at the right hand of God. Set your minds on things above, not on earthly things. For you died, and your life is now hidden with Christ in God. When Christ, who is your life, appears, then you also will appear with him in glory . . .

Therefore, as God's chosen people, holy and dearly loved, clothe yourselves with compassion, kindness, humility, gentleness and patience. Bear with each other and forgive whatever grievances you may have against one another. Forgive as the Lord forgave you. And over all these virtues put on love, which binds them all together in perfect unity.

COLOSSIANS 3:1-4, 12-14

One summer afternoon I climbed a hill near my home. When I reached the top, I stretched out on the grass to relax.

Turning my head to one side, my eyes focused on some blades of grass within inches of my face. This short-range focus not only strained my eyes, but it also blurred my view of anything beyond the end of my nose! So I began to adjust my focus, and then the distant city came into view instead.

I found I could shift my sights from near to far at will. The choice was mine.

In Colossians 3, the apostle Paul emphasized that followers of Christ need to be heavenly-minded, not earthly-minded (vv. 1–2). We can choose which it will be.

We can succumb to selfish, earthbound thoughts, blurring our view of anything beyond the end of our noses. Or we can gaze through this sinful scene and fix our attention on things above, where Christ is seated at God's right hand—and we with Him! Then, and only then, are we in a position to see what's most important in life.

Only the mind that's set on things above can say no to sin and yes to Christlike holiness. The choice is ours.

~

THE ONLY WAY TO SEE LIFE CLEARLY
IS TO FOCUS ON CHRIST.

*Because Jesus lives forever, he has a permanent priesthood.
Therefore he is able to save completely those who come to God
through him, because he always lives to intercede for them.*

*Such a high priest meets our need—one who is holy, blameless,
pure, set apart from sinners, exalted above the heavens. Unlike the
other high priests, he does not need to offer sacrifices day after day,
first for his own sins, and then for the sins of the people. He sacrificed
for their sins once for all when he offered himself. For the law
appoints as high priests men who are weak; but the oath, which came
after the law, appointed the Son, who has been made perfect forever.*

H E B R E W S   7 : 2 4 – 2 8

*I*t was dawn, and I was painfully aware of being only a few weeks into widowhood. After another restless night, I felt too weary to pray for myself. "Lord," I sighed, "I need someone to pray for me right now."

Almost instantly God's Spirit comforted my distraught mind with the words of Hebrews 7:25, reminding me that Jesus was praying for me that very moment. With a wave of relief, I acknowledged Him as my lifelong intercessor. I will never forget how that bleak morning became gold-tinged with hope. Since then, I have drawn courage and strength countless times from my faithful High Priest.

Scottish minister Robert Murray McCheyne (1813–1843) testified, "If I could hear Christ praying for me in the next room, I would not fear a million enemies. Yet distance makes no difference. He is praying for me!"

We too can draw courage and strength from Jesus. He is our priestly representative before God the Father.

Are difficult circumstances creating fear in your heart? By all means, ask others to pray for you. But don't forget to count on the prayers of Jesus Himself. By faith, hear Him praying around the clock for you, as if He were in the next room.

~

EARTH HAS NO SORROW THAT HEAVEN DOES NOT FEEL.

The days of the blameless are known to the LORD,
and their inheritance will endure forever.
In times of disaster they will not wither;
in days of famine they will enjoy plenty.
But the wicked will perish:
The LORD's enemies will be like the beauty of the fields,
they will vanish—vanish like smoke.
The wicked borrow and do not repay,
but the righteous give generously;
those the LORD blesses will inherit the land,
but those he curses will be cut off.
If the LORD delights in a man's way,
he makes his steps firm;
though he stumble, he will not fall,
for the LORD upholds him with his hand.

PSALM 37:18-24

As children, we loved hearing three words shouted in slow succession before running a race on the playground: "Ready . . . Set . . . Go!" But have you ever been running along at top speed and heard the signal: "Ready . . . Set . . . Stop"?

Howard Westlund, a busy pastor in the Chicago area, told about such an experience. In a letter to his congregation, he said, "I was ready for a full evening which would include involvement with our youth group. Then it happened: 'Ready . . . Set . . . Stop!'"

Howard was rushed to the hospital with a severe leg infection. During that time, he remembered a paraphrased version of today's text: "The Lord orders our starts and our stops." Yes, that busy pastor had been brought to an abrupt halt.

Later Pastor Westlund wrote, "I wasn't ready for a stop. How do you get ready for the thing you're not ready for? I hadn't missed a service due to sickness in twenty-five years! When God tells us to stop, we can fuss and complain and argue how much we are needed in the 'go' position. Or we can just wait, with a growing trust that He does all things well."

Howard chose the latter and learned that continuing to trust God is the only way to get ready for the things we're not ready for. Have you learned that vital lesson?

GOD CAN USE LIFE'S STOPS TO KEEP US MOVING.

THE STRONG WEAK PEOPLE

I will not boast about myself, except about my weaknesses. Even if I should choose to boast, I would not be a fool, because I would be speaking the truth. But I refrain, so no one will think more of me than is warranted by what I do or say.

To keep me from becoming conceited because of these surpassingly great revelations, there was given me a thorn in my flesh, a messenger of Satan, to torment me. Three times I pleaded with the Lord to take it away from me. But he said to me, "My grace is sufficient for you, for my power is made perfect in weakness." Therefore I will boast all the more gladly about my weaknesses, so that Christ's power may rest on me. That is why, for Christ's sake, I delight in weaknesses, in insults, in hardships, in persecutions, in difficulties. For when I am weak, then I am strong.

2 CORINTHIANS 12:5-10

*I*f there is anything that we love to hate more than the arrogance of others, it would have to be an awareness of our own weakness. We detest it so much that we invent ways to cover our personal inadequacy.

Even the apostle Paul needed to be reminded of his own frailty. He was jabbed time and again by a "thorn in the flesh" (2 Corinthians 12:7). He didn't name his thorn, but J. Oswald Sanders reminds us that whatever it was, "it hurt, humiliated, and restricted Paul." Three times he begged the Lord to take it away, but his request was not granted. Instead, he used his thorn to tap into God's all-sufficient grace. The Lord promised, "My grace is sufficient for you, for my power is made perfect in weakness" (v. 9).

Courageously, Paul began to "own" his weakness and put the Lord's grace to the test, a pathway that Sanders calls "a gradual educative process" in the apostle's life. Sanders notes that eventually Paul no longer regarded his thorn as a "limiting handicap" but as a "heavenly advantage." And his advantage was this: When he was weak in himself, he was strong in the Lord.

As we accept our weaknesses, in Christ we can be strong weak people.

TO KNOW GOD'S STRENGTH,
WE MUST KNOW OUR WEAKNESS.

Through Jesus, therefore, let us continually offer to God a sacrifice of praise—the fruit of lips that confess his name. And do not forget to do good and to share with others, for with such sacrifices God is pleased.

Obey your leaders and submit to their authority. They keep watch over you as men who must give an account. Obey them so that their work will be a joy, not a burden, for that would be of no advantage to you.

Pray for us. We are sure that we have a clear conscience and desire to live honorably in every way. I particularly urge you to pray so that I may be restored to you soon.

May the God of peace, who through the blood of the eternal covenant brought back from the dead our Lord Jesus, that great Shepherd of the sheep, equip you with everything good for doing his will, and may he work in us what is pleasing to him, through Jesus Christ, to whom be glory for ever and ever. Amen.

HEBREWS 13:15–21

*P*eople who have roast preacher for Sunday dinner need a change of diet. And a pastor who verbally chews up his congregation needs to look again at his mission. A caring preacher will build up his church, and a caring church will build up its preacher.

In Hebrews 13:17, church leaders are called to watch over their flock as those who must give an account before God. That's a tall order, but it's what God appoints them to do. And in the same verse, members of the congregation are reminded of their responsibility. They are told to let their leaders be leaders. They are to be submissive to them and open to their correction so that their leaders will have joy rather than grief as they seek to be faithful in carrying out their God-appointed duties.

How tragic that many congregations have never learned this! Six days a week they may criticize their pastor and on the seventh listen negatively as he preaches his heart out. Then they go home and have their favorite Sunday dinner—not fried chicken, but roast preacher.

Whatever our place in the body of Christ, let's build others up through mutual caring. Then instead of devouring one another, we will find joy in seeing pastors and their people being nourished and fed by one another.

<hr />

PASTORS WHO PREACH GOD'S WORD
NEED A GOOD WORD FROM GOD'S PEOPLE.

Praise the LORD.
Praise, O servants of the LORD,
*   praise the name of the LORD.*
Let the name of the LORD be praised,
*   both now and forevermore.*
From the rising of the sun to the place where it sets,
*   the name of the LORD is to be praised.*
The LORD is exalted over all the nations,
*   his glory above the heavens.*
Who is like the LORD our God,
*   the One who sits enthroned on high,*
who stoops down to look
*   on the heavens and the earth?*

He raises the poor from the dust
*   and lifts the needy from the ash heap;*
he seats them with princes,
*   with the princes of their people.*
He settles the barren woman in her home
*   as a happy mother of children.*

Praise the LORD.

PSALM 113

For several years I've worked in a ministry to drug addicts, and I've seen Christ transform many who had lost hope. Yet in response to a newspaper article about our work, I received a letter from someone who said, "You are wasting your time working with worthless drug addicts. They should be given a lethal injection and tossed on the city dump."

How heartless! These people need a massive dose of good news. They (and also that letter writer) need to hear that God doesn't cast us sinners off on some trash heap. On the contrary, He loved this world so much that He sent His only Son to die for our sins. And whoever puts his faith in Him will not perish, but will be given eternal life (John 3:16).

Some people visit dumps, searching for objects to redeem and restore. According to Psalm 113, God looks compassionately on human castaways. He seeks ways to lift them out of the ash heaps of sin and death and to give them a place of honor and dignity (vv. 7–8).

If that is God's response to this world's castaways, we should make it ours. We too were lost in the depths of sin but were raised to newness of life. God says of sinners, "No dumping allowed!"

～

CHRIST WAS LIFTED UP ON THE CROSS
THAT WE MIGHT BE LIFTED OUT OF OUR SIN.

Remember the days of old;
consider the generations long past.
Ask your father and he will tell you,
your elders, and they will explain to you.
When the Most High gave the nations their inheritance,
when he divided all mankind,
he set up boundaries for the peoples
according to the number of the sons of Israel.
For the LORD's portion is his people,
Jacob his allotted inheritance.
In a desert land he found him,
in a barren and howling waste.
He shielded him and cared for him;
he guarded him as the apple of his eye,
like an eagle that stirs up its nest
and hovers over its young,
that spreads its wings to catch them
and carries them on its pinions.
The LORD alone led him;
no foreign god was with him.

DEUTERONOMY 32:7–12

*I*n the tender song of Moses found in Deuteronomy 32, God is portrayed as a dedicated mother eagle who can be trusted by her young, even in the scary experience of learning to fly (v. 11).

A mother eagle builds a comfortable nest for her young, padding it with feathers from her own breast. But the God-given instinct that builds that secure nest also forces the eaglets out of it before long. Eagles are made to fly, and love will not fail to teach them. Only then will they become what they are meant to be.

So one day the mother eagle will disturb the twigs of the nest, making it an uncomfortable place to stay. Then she will pick up a perplexed eaglet, soar into the sky, and drop it. The little bird will begin to free fall. Where is Mama now? She is not far away. Quickly she will swoop under and catch the fledgling on one strong wing. She will repeat this exercise until each eaglet is capable of flying on its own.

Are you afraid of free falling? Remember, God will fly to your rescue and spread His everlasting arms beneath you. He will also teach you something new and wonderful through it. Falling into God's arms is nothing to be afraid of.

~

GOD'S LOVE DOES NOT KEEP US FROM TRIALS
BUT SEES US THROUGH THEM.

As they approached Jerusalem and came to Bethphage on the Mount of Olives, Jesus sent two disciples, saying to them, "Go to the village ahead of you, and at once you will find a donkey tied there, with her colt by her. Untie them and bring them to me. If anyone says anything to you, tell him that the Lord needs them, and he will send them right away."

This took place to fulfill what was spoken through the prophet:

> *"Say to the Daughter of Zion,*
> *'See, your king comes to you,*
> *gentle and riding on a donkey,*
> *on a colt, the foal of a donkey.'"*

The disciples went and did as Jesus had instructed them. They brought the donkey and the colt, placed their cloaks on them, and Jesus sat on them. A very large crowd spread their cloaks on the road, while others cut branches from the trees and spread them on the road. The crowds that went ahead of him and those that followed shouted,

> *"Hosanna to the Son of David!"*
> *"Blessed is he who comes in the name of the Lord!"*
> *"Hosanna in the highest!"*

MATTHEW 21:1–9

People often speak of donkeys in belittling terms. You may have heard the expression, "I'm just someone who has to do all the donkey work." Or "So-and-so is as stubborn as a mule" (a mule is half donkey).

These sayings overlook the contributions of a truly valuable animal. Donkeys have served the human race for thousands of years. They were once prized as symbols of humility, gentleness, and peace.

In Bible days, donkeys that had never been ridden were regarded as especially suitable for religious purposes. So it was most fitting that Jesus sent for a colt to perform the royal task of carrying Him into Jerusalem. How enviable was that donkey's mission! How like our mission as Jesus' followers!

A missionary in China calls herself "the Lord's donkey." She's a humble believer, "carrying" her Lord faithfully into town after town and training others to do likewise. The Lord has need of many such "donkeys" in today's world, humble people who will carry Him into their Jerusalem and make Him known.

Just as the donkey was untied for use by Jesus (Mark 11:4–5), we too must be released from worldly attachments so we can serve Christ. Are we willing to do donkey work?

~~

HUMBLE WORK BECOMES HOLY WORK
WHEN IT'S DONE FOR GOD.

But whatever was to my profit I now consider loss for the sake of Christ. What is more, I consider everything a loss compared to the surpassing greatness of knowing Christ Jesus my Lord, for whose sake I have lost all things. I consider them rubbish, that I may gain Christ and be found in him, not having a righteousness of my own that comes from the law, but that which is through faith in Christ—the righteousness that comes from God and is by faith. I want to know Christ and the power of his resurrection and the fellowship of sharing in his sufferings, becoming like him in his death, and so, somehow, to attain to the resurrection from the dead.

Not that I have already obtained all this, or have already been made perfect, but I press on to take hold of that for which Christ Jesus took hold of me.

PHILIPPIANS 3:7-12

urry up!" "You're too slow!" "We're late!" How often do impatient words like these crop up in our speech, revealing our fast pace of life? If we're not careful, we become people living in the fast lane, demanding quick arrivals and instant results. Stress experts call this problem "hurry sickness."

In Philippians 3, the apostle Paul's testimony of lifelong growth reminds us that Christian maturity can be encouraged but not hurried. In his book *Overcomers Through the Cross*, Paul Billheimer says that just as God takes time to make an oak tree, He takes time to make a saint. Christian growth is a process.

Billheimer writes, "An unripe apple is not fit to eat, but we should not therefore condemn it. It is not yet ready for eating because God is not done making it. It is a phase of its career and good in its place."

Are you feeling impatient over your spiritual growth? Remember, God is not finished with you—nor does He expect to be until He calls you home. Only make sure that your goal is to know Christ and to become more like Him. Then slowly but surely, under blue skies and stormy, He will bring you to maturity. It's His sure cure for "hurry sickness."

~~

THERE ARE NO SHORTCUTS TO SPIRITUAL MATURITY.

I am the true vine, and my Father is the gardener. He cuts off every branch in me that bears no fruit, while every branch that does bear fruit he prunes so that it will be even more fruitful. You are already clean because of the word I have spoken to you. Remain in me, and I will remain in you. No branch can bear fruit by itself; it must remain in the vine. Neither can you bear fruit unless you remain in me.

I am the vine; you are the branches. If a man remains in me and I in him, he will bear much fruit; apart from me you can do nothing. If anyone does not remain in me, he is like a branch that is thrown away and withers; such branches are picked up, thrown into the fire and burned. If you remain in me and my words remain in you, ask whatever you wish, and it will be given you. This is to my Father's glory, that you bear much fruit, showing yourselves to be my disciples."

JOHN 15:1–8

Almost every woman likes to receive a bouquet of cut flowers. After admiring and smelling them, she wastes no time getting them into water. Even though fresh and beautiful when she gets them, their days are numbered. Because they've been severed from their life source, they will soon wither and die. One day she will have to throw them away.

Author Lloyd Ogilvie sees in this a picture of the Christian whose spiritual vitality has faded and shriveled. Such a person has become a "cut-flower Christian." This is similar to the illustration Jesus used in describing the vine and the branches. Just as a branch can't bear fruit by itself, He explained, we can't bear spiritual fruit unless we abide in Him, the true vine (John 15:4).

If a branch could speak, it wouldn't apologize for its need to depend on the vine for bearing fruit. It would say instead, "For this I was made!" Jesus likewise knew we were made for dependence on Him, our life source—no apology needed! In fact, such dependence is the only way to avoid becoming a "cut-flower Christian."

Let's embrace His declaration, "Without Me you can do nothing." He is really saying, "With Me you can do everything I appoint for you, including bearing much fruit!"

~

FELLOWSHIP WITH CHRIST
IS THE SECRET OF FRUITFULNESS.

Jesus said to them, "If God were your Father, you would love me, for I came from God and now am here. I have not come on my own; but he sent me. Why is my language not clear to you? Because you are unable to hear what I say. You belong to your father, the devil, and you want to carry out your father's desire. He was a murderer from the beginning, not holding to the truth, for there is no truth in him. When he lies, he speaks his native language, for he is a liar and the father of lies. Yet because I tell the truth, you do not believe me! Can any of you prove me guilty of sin? If I am telling the truth, why don't you believe me? He who belongs to God hears what God says. The reason you do not hear is that you do not belong to God."

JOHN 8:42–47

Communication—everybody's discussing it, studying it, practicing it. Yet despite our improved communication skills, we may feel like the author who wrote, "I know that you believe you understand what you think I said, but I am not sure you realize that what you heard is not what I meant."

Good communication involves more than good speaking; it also requires good listening.

Jesus, the master communicator, was often misunderstood, as we see in today's Scripture. Although He spoke the truth clearly, His hearers jumbled up His message and then rejected it. "Why is my language not clear to you?" He quizzed them. Answering His own question, He replied, "Because you are unable to hear what I say" (John 8:43). Why were they such poor listeners? Not because Jesus failed to communicate, but because they didn't want to hear the truth. And why didn't they? Because it made them face up to their need to change.

When we say, "God is getting through to me," it's not because He's communicating better but because we're hearing and willing to change. Let's always make listening to God one of our best communication skills.

～～～

IT'S HARD TO TUNE IN ON HEAVEN'S MESSAGE
IF OUR LIVES ARE FULL OF EARTHLY STATIC.

Find rest, O my soul, in God alone;
  my hope comes from him.
He alone is my rock and my salvation;
  he is my fortress, I will not be shaken.
My salvation and my honor depend on God;
  he is my mighty rock, my refuge.
Trust in him at all times, O people;
  pour out your hearts to him,
  for God is our refuge.
    Selah
Lowborn men are but a breath,
  the highborn are but a lie;
  if weighed on a balance, they are nothing;
  together they are only a breath.
Do not trust in extortion
  or take pride in stolen goods;
  though your riches increase,
  do not set your heart on them.
One thing God has spoken,
  two things have I heard:
  that you, O God, are strong,
and that you, O Lord, are loving.
  Surely you will reward each person
  according to what he has done.

PSALM 62:5-12

We would expect King David to be extremely upset because his enemies were scheming to dethrone him. Yet in Psalm 62 he testified that his soul was quietly confident before God. How was this possible in the midst of such turmoil? Verse 8 offers a clue—one I discovered for myself several years ago.

I had just returned home, battle-weary, alone, and at my wit's end. As I began pouring out my woes before God, I suddenly stopped myself and said, "Father, forgive me. I'm treating You like a counselor!" But the torrent of words flowed on, followed by the same embarrassing apology. Then God's Spirit whispered deep within, "I am your Great Counselor."

But of course! Hadn't He, the Creator of my physical and spiritual makeup, also created my emotions? How reasonable, then, to spread out my ragged feelings before Him. Then came His comforting, corrective counsel, ministered skillfully by the Holy Spirit through His Word. My problems didn't evaporate, but like David, I could rest in God alone. I was at peace again.

Never hesitate to pour out your heart to God. In your day of trouble, you'll find that prayer is the shortest route between your heart and God's.

GOD FILLS OUR HEART WITH PEACE
WHEN WE POUR OUT OUR HEART TO HIM.

By the grace God has given me, I laid a foundation as an expert builder, and someone else is building on it. But each one should be careful how he builds. For no one can lay any foundation other than the one already laid, which is Jesus Christ. If any man builds on this foundation using gold, silver, costly stones, wood, hay or straw, his work will be shown for what it is, because the Day will bring it to light. It will be revealed with fire, and the fire will test the quality of each man's work. If what he has built survives, he will receive his reward. If it is burned up, he will suffer loss; he himself will be saved, but only as one escaping through the flames.

1 CORINTHIANS 3:10–15

*E*veryone in the community knew Carl. He was a farmer and family man whose dedication went beyond his own productive fields. He also was known for his greater dedication to what he called "God's harvest field."

Carl's neighbors sometimes considered him foolish, especially over his reluctance to work on Sundays. Instead, he would go to church, visit shut-ins, and focus on family life. Choosing God's priorities over crop priorities seemed foolhardy.

One Sunday, while neighbors hastily gathered their harvest before a predicted storm, Carl went to church as usual. Later a neighbor mocked, "Think, Carl, by the end of the month the rest of us will be enjoying a big payoff because of our work. But you may end up with nothing, all because of your work for God. Where will you be then?" With quiet confidence, Carl replied, "Working for God has a payoff too, but not necessarily at the end of the month. The question is, when that day comes, where will you be?"

Which payday takes priority in your life? The one at the end of the month or the day you stand before Christ? Now is the time to evaluate your goals in life, for one day the Lord will reward the wise choices you've made.

~~~

SERVING THE LORD IS AN INVESTMENT
THAT PAYS ETERNAL DIVIDENDS.

I have hidden your word in my heart
that I might not sin against you.
Do good to your servant, and I will live;
I will obey your word.
Open my eyes that I may see
wonderful things in your law.
I am a stranger on earth;
do not hide your commands from me.
My soul is consumed with longing
for your laws at all times.
You rebuke the arrogant, who are cursed
and who stray from your commands.
Remove from me scorn and contempt,
for I keep your statutes.
Though rulers sit together and slander me,
your servant will meditate on your decrees.
Your statutes are my delight;
they are my counselors.

PSALM 119:11, 17–24

I love the sight of cows lying in the field, chewing their cud. But what is cud? And why do they spend so much time chewing it?

Cows first fill their stomachs with grass and other food. Then they settle down for a good, long chew. They bring the food back up from their stomachs and rework what they've already eaten, assimilating its goodness and transforming it into rich milk. Time-consuming? Yes. A waste of time? Not if they want to give good milk.

The phrase "chewing the cud" is used to describe the process of meditation. The writer of Psalm 119 obviously did a lot of mental chewing as he read God's Word. No fast food for him! If we follow his example of careful and prayerful Scripture reading, we will

- Be strengthened against sin (v. 11).
- Find delight in learning more about God (vv. 15–16).
- Discover wonderful spiritual truths (v. 18).
- Find wise counsel for daily living (v. 24).

Meditation is more than reading the Bible and believing it. It's applying Scripture to everyday life.

God's Word is not meant to be fast food. Take time for a good long chew.

~~~

TO BE A HEALTHY CHRISTIAN,
DON'T TREAT THE BIBLE AS SNACK FOOD.

So then, just as you received Christ Jesus as Lord, continue to live in him, rooted and built up in him, strengthened in the faith as you were taught, and overflowing with thankfulness.

See to it that no one takes you captive through hollow and deceptive philosophy, which depends on human tradition and the basic principles of this world rather than on Christ.

For in Christ all the fullness of the Deity lives in bodily form, and you have been given fullness in Christ, who is the head over every power and authority.

COLOSSIANS 2:6–10

A friend of mine, Elizabeth-Ann, is in her sixties, single, and radiantly contented. "But how is that possible?" she is often asked. To answer this question she wrote a book titled *Complete as One*, which is based on Colossians 2:10. She recalls being challenged years ago by a comment about a friend: "You know what I appreciate about June? She's so satisfied with Christ."

That phrase, "satisfied with Christ," left a profound impact on Elizabeth-Ann. She was twenty-one at the time and had been converted three years earlier. Her friends were getting engaged and married, and she was happy for them. But she was hearing comments like, "Have you seen how radiant Mary is?" and "I've never seen John so happy." This set her to thinking: These friends are Christians. Certainly it is appropriate for them to radiate happiness, but why do they have to get a partner before they experience the joy and fulfillment Christians should have? So she began praying, "Lord, I don't want to marry until I have learned to be satisfied with You."

Even though Elizabeth-Ann is still single, she believes that God has answered her prayer. She is rooted and built up in Christ. And that's the key to completeness—whether married or single.

~~~

FOR LASTING SATISFACTION, PUT GOD'S WILL FIRST.

"Look at the birds of the air; they do not sow or reap or store away in barns, and yet your heavenly Father feeds them. Are you not much more valuable than they? Who of you by worrying can add a single hour to his life?

"And why do you worry about clothes? See how the lilies of the field grow. They do not labor or spin. Yet I tell you that not even Solomon in all his splendor was dressed like one of these. If that is how God clothes the grass of the field, which is here today and tomorrow is thrown into the fire, will he not much more clothe you, O you of little faith? So do not worry, saying, 'What shall we eat?' or 'What shall we drink?' or 'What shall we wear?' For the pagans run after all these things, and your heavenly Father knows that you need them. But seek first his kingdom and his righteousness, and all these things will be given to you as well. Therefore do not worry about tomorrow, for tomorrow will worry about itself. Each day has enough trouble of its own."

MATTHEW 6:26–34

*W*e often wish we could see what lies around the corner in life. Then we could prepare for it, control it, or avoid it.

A wise person has said, "Though we can't see around corners, God can!" How much better and more reassuring that is!

Recently my ten-year-old granddaughter Emily and I were boiling eggs for breakfast. As we stared into the boiling water and wondered how long it would take to get the eggs just right, Emily said, "Pity we can't open them up to see how they're doing." I agreed! But that would have spoiled them, so we had to rely on guesswork, with no guarantee of results.

We began talking about other things we would like to see but can't—like tomorrow. Too bad we can't crack tomorrow open, we said, to see if it's the way we would like it. But meddling with tomorrow before its time, like opening a partly cooked egg, would spoil both today and tomorrow.

Because Jesus has promised to care for us every day—and that includes tomorrow—we can live by faith one day at a time (Matthew 6:33–34).

Emily and I decided to leave tomorrow safely in God's hands. Have you?

~~~

YOU'RE ONLY COOKING UP TROUBLE
WHEN YOU STEW ABOUT TOMORROW.

One day as Jesus was standing by the Lake of Gennesaret, with the people crowding around him and listening to the word of God, he saw at the water's edge two boats, left there by the fishermen, who were washing their nets. He got into one of the boats, the one belonging to Simon, and asked him to put out a little from shore. Then he sat down and taught the people from the boat.

When he had finished speaking, he said to Simon, "Put out into deep water, and let down the nets for a catch."

Simon answered, "Master, we've worked hard all night and haven't caught anything. But because you say so, I will let down the nets."

When they had done so, they caught such a large number of fish that their nets began to break. So they signaled their partners in the other boat to come and help them, and they came and filled both boats so full that they began to sink.

When Simon Peter saw this, he fell at Jesus' knees and said, "Go away from me, Lord; I am a sinful man!" For he and all his companions were astonished at the catch of fish they had taken, and so were James and John, the sons of Zebedee, Simon's partners.

Then Jesus said to Simon, "Don't be afraid; from now on you will catch men." So they pulled their boats up on shore, left everything and followed him.

LUKE 5:1–11

Have you ever raced around the supermarket, praying you won't see someone you know because you're too hurried to stop? I have. And yet we should always be available for the opportunities God gives us to witness.

Author Gladys Hunt has written, "When Jesus walked by the Sea of Galilee, He called simple fishermen and said, 'Come, follow Me, and I will make you fishers of men' (Matthew 4:19). They left their nets and followed Him. These men knew the excitement of the catch. And they knew Jesus could involve them in something far bigger than catching fish. Our difficulty is that we have forgotten the excitement of the catch, if indeed we ever knew it."

If we're to experience the joy of "catching" people for Christ, we must go out among them and sincerely befriend them. But as important as witnessing is, don't be a friend just to witness; rather, witness because you are a friend. As someone has said, "People don't care how much you know until they know how much you care!"

Will you be doing any shopping today? Be looking for opportunities to witness. The joy of a catch may be in the next aisle.

~~~

YOU WON'T FIND OPPORTUNITIES TO WITNESS
IF YOU'RE NOT LOOKING FOR THEM.

Then Job replied:

I have heard many things like these;
miserable comforters are you all!
Will your long-winded speeches never end?
What ails you that you keep on arguing?
I also could speak like you,
if you were in my place;
I could make fine speeches against you
and shake my head at you.
But my mouth would encourage you;
comfort from my lips would bring you relief.
Yet if I speak, my pain is not relieved;
and if I refrain, it does not go away.

JOB 16:1-6

*I*n her book *Listening to Others*, Joyce Huggett relates her experiences of listening to suffering people. She says they often raved about all she had done for them. "On many occasions," she writes, "I had not 'done' anything. I had 'just listened.' I quickly came to the conclusion that 'just listening' was indeed an effective way of helping others."

This was the help that Job's wordy, preachy friends failed to give him. He complained that they were "miserable comforters" (Job 16:2) and was so distraught that he even accused God of not listening. He cried out, "Oh, that I had someone to hear me!" (31:35).

What does active listening accomplish? Listening is a way of loving others. It says, "I want to understand and know you." It comforts the brokenhearted, builds relationships, and encourages faith in God. Listening is also a means of learning the facts. Solomon, in Proverbs 18:13, warned that it is folly to answer a matter before hearing it.

Most of all, listening to others should reflect our attentiveness toward God and His Word. He has so much He wants to teach us and tell us. As you take a moment of stillness today and give Him a listening ear, you'll be better able to listen to the hurting people around you.

~~

YOU CAN WIN MORE FRIENDS WITH YOUR EARS
THAN WITH YOUR MOUTH.

The fear of the LORD is pure,
  enduring forever.
The ordinances of the LORD are sure
  and altogether righteous.
They are more precious than gold,
  than much pure gold;
they are sweeter than honey,
  than honey from the comb.
By them is your servant warned;
  in keeping them there is great reward.
Who can discern his errors?
  Forgive my hidden faults.
Keep your servant also from willful sins;
  may they not rule over me.
Then will I be blameless,
  innocent of great transgression.
May the words of my mouth and the meditation of my heart
  be pleasing in your sight,
    O LORD, my Rock and my Redeemer.

PSALM 19:9–14

A humorous greeting card showed a grotesquely thin cow wandering in a barren desert. The skinny cow was meant to illustrate "where nonfat milk comes from." The logic of the cartoon, of course, is entirely unscientific. Nonfat milk is not produced by nonfat cows!

The idea, however, reminds me of D. L. Moody's comment: "Most people talk cream and live skim milk." If our hearts are spiritually underfed, we will produce "skim-milk" Christianity. Our lips may utter spiritual-sounding words in prayer, worship, and conversation, giving the impression of "top-grade cream." But the reality is revealed by what is consistently produced in our lives.

How can we live cream and not just talk it? David grappled with this in Psalm 19. In verses 12 and 13 he was honest with himself and with God when he asked to be cleansed from secret faults and presumptuous sins. Beyond forgiveness, David knew he needed God's continuing strength and help to harmonize his walk with his talk. So he earnestly prayed, "May the words of my mouth and the meditation of my heart be acceptable in Your sight, O LORD, my Rock and my Redeemer" (v. 14).

In our walk, let's move from skim milk to cream by being open, honest, and prayerful.

~~~

OUR WORDS AND OUR DEEDS
SHOULD SAY THE SAME THING.

When Jesus looked up and saw a great crowd coming toward him, he said to Philip, "Where shall we buy bread for these people to eat?" He asked this only to test him, for he already had in mind what he was going to do.

Philip answered him, "Eight months' wages would not buy enough bread for each one to have a bite!"

Another of his disciples, Andrew, Simon Peter's brother, spoke up, "Here is a boy with five small barley loaves and two small fish, but how far will they go among so many?"

Jesus said, "Have the people sit down." There was plenty of grass in that place, and the men sat down, about five thousand of them. Jesus then took the loaves, gave thanks, and distributed to those who were seated as much as they wanted. He did the same with the fish.

When they had all had enough to eat, he said to his disciples, "Gather the pieces that are left over. Let nothing be wasted." So they gathered them and filled twelve baskets with the pieces of the five barley loaves left over by those who had eaten.

After the people saw the miraculous sign that Jesus did, they began to say, "Surely this is the Prophet who is to come into the world."

JOHN 6:5–14

While I was leading a seminar, I passed around a loaf of unsliced bread and asked each person to respond to it. One squeezed it and said, "It's fresh." Another commented, "It smells delicious." Still another noted, "It looks nourishing."

Finally someone said, "That's true, but I'm hungry!" With that, she broke off a piece and ate it. Her response said it all: Unbroken bread is useless.

One day Jesus faced five thousand hungry people. Only by breaking the five loaves and two fish into pieces could He miraculously feed the multitude (John 6:11), and He refused to waste any leftover fragments (v. 12).

Not only did this miracle foreshadow Christ's brokenness on the cross—a breaking that would make the Bread of Life available to all—but it also speaks to me of the brokenness that believers must experience if they are to be used by God.

Do you fear a loss of usefulness due to broken health, broken hopes, broken promises? Fear not! Although some things lose their usefulness once they're broken, there are two things that become more useful: broken loaves and broken lives.

If you'll yield the fragments of your life to God, He'll not waste a crumb of what you're going through.

~~~

BROKEN THINGS BECOME USEFUL IN GOD'S HANDS.

When they came to the crowd, a man approached Jesus and knelt before him. "Lord, have mercy on my son," he said. "He has seizures and is suffering greatly. He often falls into the fire or into the water. I brought him to your disciples, but they could not heal him."

"O unbelieving and perverse generation," Jesus replied, "how long shall I stay with you? How long shall I put up with you? Bring the boy here to me." Jesus rebuked the demon, and it came out of the boy, and he was healed from that moment.

Then the disciples came to Jesus in private and asked, "Why couldn't we drive it out?"

He replied, "Because you have so little faith. I tell you the truth, if you have faith as small as a mustard seed, you can say to this mountain, 'Move from here to there' and it will move. Nothing will be impossible for you."

MATTHEW 17:14–20

*F*aith—we all wish we had more of it, especially when facing mountainous problems. Yet most of us are well practiced in faith. We sit down in chairs without checking them out; we use microwave ovens without analyzing how they work; we put keys in doors and expect them to open. We don't go around moaning, "If only I had more faith in chairs, in microwaves, in keys." We depend on these objects because we see them as reliable—not because we've worked up great feelings of confidence.

Jesus didn't say to His disciples, "Have more faith in God." He simply said, "Have faith in God" (Mark 11:22).

Bible teacher Stuart Briscoe writes, "Faith is only as valid as its object. You could have tremendous faith in very thin ice and drown . . . You could have very little faith in very thick ice and be perfectly secure."

Many Christians have faith in faith rather than faith in God. When facing trials, they agonize to attain mountain-size faith. But Jesus taught that faith the size of a mustard seed is sufficient, if planted in the soil of God's greatness.

What is your mountain today? As soon as you plant your mustard seed of faith in God, your mountain becomes His responsibility—and you can rest in His faithfulness.

~

HAVE FAITH IN GOD—NOT FAITH IN FAITH.

Keep on loving each other as brothers. Do not forget to entertain strangers, for by so doing some people have entertained angels without knowing it. Remember those in prison as if you were their fellow prisoners, and those who are mistreated as if you yourselves were suffering . . .

Through Jesus, therefore, let us continually offer to God a sacrifice of praise—the fruit of lips that confess his name. And do not forget to do good and to share with others, for with such sacrifices God is pleased.

HEBREWS 13:1-3, 15-16

*D*uring His life on earth, Jesus chose to identify with poor and destitute people. He lived as one who had no place to call home (Matthew 8:20), and His ministry was marked by compassion for the needy.

In her book *Hidden Art*, Edith Schaeffer of L'Abri Fellowship tells of feeding the occasional vagrant who would stop at her back door and ask, "May I have a cup of coffee, ma'am, and maybe some bread?"

Edith would invite him to sit down, then go in to prepare a tray of food fit for a king: steaming soup and thick sandwiches, cut and arranged artfully on a plate with garnishes. The children would make a tiny bouquet, and if it was dusk they would add a candle. In amazement the man would gasp, "For me?"

"Yes," Edith would answer, "and coffee will be ready in a minute. This Gospel of John is for you too. Take it with you. It really is very important."

In my kitchen hangs this saying: "Food is God's love made edible." Certainly those vagrants at Edith's door experienced God's love through her and her family.

How about serving up God's love to someone? Through your generosity you will be serving Christ—and perhaps you may be serving an angel in disguise (Hebrews 13:2).

~~~

FOOD IS GOD'S LOVE MADE EDIBLE.

THE ADVANTAGE OF WEAKNESS

I must go on boasting. Although there is nothing to be gained, I will go on to visions and revelations from the Lord. I know a man in Christ who fourteen years ago was caught up to the third heaven. Whether it was in the body or out of the body I do not know—God knows. And I know that this man—whether in the body or apart from the body I do not know, but God knows—was caught up to paradise. He heard inexpressible things, things that man is not permitted to tell. I will boast about a man like that, but I will not boast about myself, except about my weaknesses. Even if I should choose to boast, I would not be a fool, because I would be speaking the truth. But I refrain, so no one will think more of me than is warranted by what I do or say.

To keep me from becoming conceited because of these surpassingly great revelations, there was given me a thorn in my flesh, a messenger of Satan, to torment me. Three times I pleaded with the Lord to take it away from me. But he said to me, "My grace is sufficient for you, for my power is made perfect in weakness." Therefore I will boast all the more gladly about my weaknesses, so that Christ's power may rest on me. That is why, for Christ's sake, I delight in weaknesses, in insults, in hardships, in persecutions, in difficulties. For when I am weak, then I am strong.

2 CORINTHIANS 12:1–10

*I*t is always a joy to talk with my old college friend Tom and get caught up on what the Lord has been teaching us since we last met.

One time Tom began with a sheepish grin, "You know, I can't believe how many years it's taken me to learn my latest lesson—and I'm a Bible teacher!" He went on to list some of the trials and testings he and his family had been facing and how unworthy he felt teaching an adult Sunday school class. "Week after week I felt I was a total failure," he confided, "and kept wondering if this might be my last Sunday before announcing my resignation."

Then one Sunday Tom noticed a young woman who stayed behind to speak to him. She was a friend of his family, so she knew what they had been going through. "Tom," she said, "I hope you won't take this the wrong way, but you're a much better teacher when you're going through tough times!"

Another sheepish grin crept across Tom's face as he told me, "Only then did I feel I grasped the Lord's response to Paul's thorn in the flesh: 'My grace is sufficient for you, for My power is made perfect in weakness.'"

Weakness helps us to relate to others and lets God's power work in our lives. That may be our greatest asset.

~

WE MAY FACE SITUATIONS BEYOND OUR RESERVES,
BUT NEVER BEYOND GOD'S RESOURCES.

DARTBOARD OR PIPELINE?

Now I rejoice in what was suffered for you, and I fill up in my flesh what is still lacking in regard to Christ's afflictions, for the sake of his body, which is the church. I have become its servant by the commission God gave me to present to you the word of God in its fullness—the mystery that has been kept hidden for ages and generations, but is now disclosed to the saints. To them God has chosen to make known among the Gentiles the glorious riches of this mystery, which is Christ in you, the hope of glory.

We proclaim him, admonishing and teaching everyone with all wisdom, so that we may present everyone perfect in Christ. To this end I labor, struggling with all his energy, which so powerfully works in me.

COLOSSIANS 1:24–29

One day during my devotional time, this thought came to my mind: "Don't let life happen to you. Let life happen through you."

The first phrase described me to a T, for I tended to see life as something coming at me. I felt like a worn-out dartboard. I was using all my energies to shield myself from the darts of life's trials.

But the second phrase, "Let life happen through you," presented a different approach. Instead of dodging life's fiery darts, I was to let God's life and love be channeled through me, blessing me on its way to blessing others.

Instead of being life's dartboard, I chose that day to become God's pipeline. Then I could begin living more effectively for Him.

Some days I revert to being a dartboard, but I soon run out of the love and power to bless others. Then through confession, faith, and obedience, I reconnect myself to my heavenly supply center and resume pipeline living.

In his letter to the Colossians, Paul mentioned the many troubles he was facing. Yet he was determined to be a channel of blessing by allowing God to work through him.

What about you? Are you a dartboard or a pipeline? It's a God-given challenge and choice for every believer.

~

GOD BLESSES YOU TO BLESS OTHERS.

But now, this is what the L ORD says—
    he who created you, O Jacob,
    he who formed you, O Israel:
"Fear not, for I have redeemed you;
    I have summoned you by name; you are mine.
When you pass through the waters,
    I will be with you;
and when you pass through the rivers,
    they will not sweep over you.
When you walk through the fire,
    you will not be burned;
    the flames will not set you ablaze.
For I am the L ORD, your God,
    the Holy One of Israel, your Savior."

ISAIAH 43:1–3

I'll never forget my first experience using an automatic carwash. Approaching it with the dread of going to the dentist, I pushed the money into the slot, nervously checked and rechecked my windows, eased the car up to the line, and waited. Powers beyond my control began moving my car forward as if on a conveyor belt. With me cocooned inside, a thunderous rush of water, shampoo, and brushes hit my car from all directions. *What if I get stuck in here or water crashes in?* I thought irrationally. Suddenly the waters ceased. After a blow-dry, my car was propelled into the outside world again, clean and polished.

In the midst of all this, I remembered stormy times in my life when it seemed I was on a conveyor belt, a victim of forces beyond my control. "Carwash experiences," I now call them. I remembered that whenever I passed through deep waters, my Redeemer had been with me, sheltering me against the rising tide. When I came out on the other side, which I always did, I was able to say with joy and confidence that He is a faithful God!

Are you in the middle of a carwash experience? Trust God to bring you through to the other side. You'll then be a shining testimony of His keeping power.

~~~

WHEN YOU COME THROUGH THE TUNNEL OF TESTING,
YOU'LL SHINE BRIGHTER FOR THE LORD.

To the Jews who had believed him, Jesus said, "If you hold to my teaching, you are really my disciples. Then you will know the truth, and the truth will set you free."

They answered him, "We are Abraham's descendants and have never been slaves of anyone. How can you say that we shall be set free?"

Jesus replied, "I tell you the truth, everyone who sins is a slave to sin. Now a slave has no permanent place in the family, but a son belongs to it forever. So if the Son sets you free, you will be free indeed.

JOHN 8:31-36

here, but for the grace of God, go I." How often I've said that—especially when observing drug-addicted people. I think I say it humbly—but am I really sincere?

In John 8, Jesus told His listeners that His truth could make them free (v. 32). But weren't they free already, they protested? So Jesus tightened the screws a bit more: "Most assuredly, I say to you, whoever commits sin is a slave of sin" (v. 34). In other words, sin is addictive. And since we're all sinners, it's the addiction of us all.

At the heart of every person's sin problem is a "self" habit that can be kicked only through Christ's help. Many recovered drug addicts have found that their "self" habit is a deeper problem than their drug habit. That certainly is Ken's story. After years of running from his problems through drugs and alcohol, he finally yielded his life to Christ. "Since then," Ken testifies, "things haven't always been smooth, but Christ has been transforming my selfish way of life. I was shocked to find that I was completely addicted to me!"

We all battle that same addiction. Instead of flippantly saying, "There, but for the grace of God, go I," we should say, "There go I." No one is an exception. We're all in need of the same grace.

~~~

GOD'S GRACE SAVES THE BEST AND THE WORST
OF SINNERS.

For this reason I kneel before the Father, from whom his whole family in heaven and on earth derives its name. I pray that out of his glorious riches he may strengthen you with power through his Spirit in your inner being, so that Christ may dwell in your hearts through faith. And I pray that you, being rooted and established in love, may have power, together with all the saints, to grasp how wide and long and high and deep is the love of Christ, and to know this love that surpasses knowledge—that you may be filled to the measure of all the fullness of God.

Now to him who is able to do immeasurably more than all we ask or imagine, according to his power that is at work within us, to him be glory in the church and in Christ Jesus throughout all generations, for ever and ever! Amen.

EPHESIANS 3:14–21

*J*ennifer had just heard a disturbing report about an increase in cases of depression among women. The report cited a related upswing in alcoholism and an increased reliance on prescription drugs.

"So what are You doing about it, Lord?" Jennifer prayed. But the more she thought about it, the more she felt that God was asking her to do something. All she could see, however, were her own limitations.

To help her think it through, she listed some reasons that were keeping her from action: shyness, fear of getting involved, lack of time, a cold heart, feelings of inadequacy, fear of failure—a daunting list!

As she finished her list, she saw that it was time to pick up her children from school. She put on her coat, then reached for her gloves. They were lying limp and useless—until she slipped her hands inside them. At that moment she realized that God didn't want her to think about her limitations. Rather, He wanted to put His power into her and work through her, just as her gloves became useful when she put her hands into them.

Why do we feel inadequate for the work God has given us? He wants to love others through us, "according to his power that is at work in us" (Ephesians 3:20).

~~~

GOD'S CALL TO A TASK
INCLUDES HIS STRENGTH TO COMPLETE IT.

As the Scripture says, "Anyone who trusts in him will never be put to shame." For there is no difference between Jew and Gentile—the same Lord is Lord of all and richly blesses all who call on him, for, "Everyone who calls on the name of the Lord will be saved."

How, then, can they call on the one they have not believed in? And how can they believe in the one of whom they have not heard? And how can they hear without someone preaching to them? And how can they preach unless they are sent? As it is written, "How beautiful are the feet of those who bring good news!"

But not all the Israelites accepted the good news. For Isaiah says, "Lord, who has believed our message?" Consequently, faith comes from hearing the message, and the message is heard through the word of Christ.

ROMANS 10:11–17

*I*n 1983 at age sixteen, an English girl began an eleven-year trek around the world—on foot! Why did she do it? She said, "I had to discover myself."

In case you think you couldn't or wouldn't undertake such a journey, a podiatrist in Washington, D.C., informs us that we already have. He claims that the average person's feet travel more than four times the earth's circumference in a lifetime.

That's a lot of walking! But where are our feet taking us, and why?

In Romans 10, Paul wrote about the feet of those who carry the gospel wherever they go (v. 15). He said that unless someone goes and tells others about Jesus, they will not hear, and they will not be saved.

With that in mind, we can walk with a cause—not to discover ourselves but to help others discover Christ. For this reason, God enlists our feet, even calling them beautiful!

But what about people like Joni Eareckson Tada who can't walk? She testifies, "I've learned that you can be in a wheelchair and still walk with Jesus!" Yes, all believers can live for Jesus wherever they go. Our lives can be a shining testimony of the power and truth of the gospel.

Where will your feet be going today? How will you spread the good news about Christ?

~~

LOVING THE LOST IS THE FIRST STEP
IN LEADING THEM TO CHRIST.

When [the rulers and elders of the people] saw the courage of Peter and John and realized that they were unschooled, ordinary men, they were astonished and they took note that these men had been with Jesus. But since they could see the man who had been healed standing there with them, there was nothing they could say. So they ordered them to withdraw from the Sanhedrin and then conferred together. "What are we going to do with these men?" they asked. "Everybody living in Jerusalem knows they have done an outstanding miracle, and we cannot deny it. But to stop this thing from spreading any further among the people, we must warn these men to speak no longer to anyone in this name."

Then they called them in again and commanded them not to speak or teach at all in the name of Jesus. But Peter and John replied, "Judge for yourselves whether it is right in God's sight to obey you rather than God. For we cannot help speaking about what we have seen and heard."

A CTS 4 : 1 3 – 2 0

While driving in rush-hour traffic one day, I found myself behind a car with a bumper sticker. It had a yellow smiley face on it with these words: Smile—Jesus Loves You.

Suddenly another car squeezed in front of the "smiley" car, forcing the driver to hit the brakes. With that, he shook his fist angrily, displaying anything but a smiley face. I felt ashamed until I remembered my own impatience as a driver. The incident reminded me that our actions and reactions, more than the display of a sticker on our car, show whether we know the Lord Jesus.

Acts 4 tells us that Peter and John faced opposition from local rulers, elders, and scribes as they proclaimed the good news of Christ. But their reaction caused their opponents to start thinking. Even though Peter and John were not highly educated, the people marveled at their bold witness and realized that these two men had been with Jesus. There was no need for a bumper sticker on the apostles' donkey—their words and deeds said it all.

Do you feel too untrained or timid to be a witness for God? If you'll spend time getting to know Jesus intimately, He'll empower you to impress others with Himself. You'll have boldness—without a bumper sticker.

~

ACTIONS SPEAK LOUDER THAN BUMPER STICKERS.

Now a man came up to Jesus and asked, "Teacher, what good thing must I do to get eternal life?"

"Why do you ask me about what is good?" Jesus replied. "There is only One who is good. If you want to enter life, obey the commandments."

"Which ones?" the man inquired.

Jesus replied, " 'Do not murder, do not commit adultery, do not steal, do not give false testimony, honor your father and mother,' and 'love your neighbor as yourself.'"

"All these I have kept," the young man said. "What do I still lack?"

Jesus answered, "If you want to be perfect, go, sell your possessions and give to the poor, and you will have treasure in heaven. Then come, follow me."

When the young man heard this, he went away sad, because he had great wealth.

Then Jesus said to his disciples, "I tell you the truth, it is hard for a rich man to enter the kingdom of heaven. Again I tell you, it is easier for a camel to go through the eye of a needle than for a rich man to enter the kingdom of God."

When the disciples heard this, they were greatly astonished and asked, "Who then can be saved?"

Jesus looked at them and said, "With man this is impossible, but with God all things are possible."

MATTHEW 19:16-26

*L*ike many young children, I had a favorite book of nursery rhymes. I particularly remember Humpty Dumpty, pictured as a big, egg-shaped creature with a painted face and skinny arms and legs, perched happily on a wall. Then he fell and broke into countless pieces. As a child, I felt the hopelessness of the situation whenever I read that they "couldn't put Humpty Dumpty together again."

Since childhood I've come to know Christ as my Savior and Lord. I've experienced Him as the great Potter, reshaping the shattered pieces of my life and the lives of others. I've had the joy of seeing many so-called hopeless drug addicts made new in Christ. As a result, I've added a line to the Humpty Dumpty nursery rhyme: "What all the king's horses and all the king's men couldn't do, the King could!"

Are you or someone dear to you feeling shattered and broken today? Remember, no one is hopeless and beyond God's saving help. Jesus said, "With God all things are possible" (Matthew 19:26).

When the broken pieces of life seem beyond hope of repair, don't give up. We have a King who can put people back together again.

~~~

NO ONE IS HOPELESS WHOSE HOPE IS IN GOD.

But Mary stood outside the tomb crying. As she wept, she bent over to look into the tomb and saw two angels in white, seated where Jesus' body had been, one at the head and the other at the foot.

They asked her, "Woman, why are you crying?"

"They have taken my Lord away," she said, "and I don't know where they have put him." At this, she turned around and saw Jesus standing there, but she did not realize that it was Jesus.

"Woman," he said, "why are you crying? Who is it you are looking for?"

Thinking he was the gardener, she said, "Sir, if you have carried him away, tell me where you have put him, and I will get him."

Jesus said to her, "Mary."

She turned toward him and cried out in Aramaic, "Rabboni!" (which means Teacher).

Jesus said, "Do not hold on to me, for I have not yet returned to the Father. Go instead to my brothers and tell them, 'I am returning to my Father and your Father, to my God and your God.' "

Mary Magdalene went to the disciples with the news: "I have seen the Lord!" And she told them that he had said these things to her.

JOHN 20:11–18

*I*t was a sunny, sad day in 1982—the day after my husband's funeral. I had gone alone to Bill's grave, hardly knowing why. As with Mary Magdalene who visited Jesus' tomb, the risen Lord was waiting for me. He impressed the words of Philippians 1:21 on my vacant mind, still numbed by Bill's untimely cancer death. I wove my prayer around the words of that verse: "For to me, to live is Christ and to die is gain."

"Lord, how often I've heard Bill testify, 'For to me, to live is Christ and to die is gain.' Well, your servant has now died, an untold loss for us, an unspeakable gain for him. I know, Lord, that I too will die someday and enter that gain. But right now I'm still alive. I know I must not live in the past, precious as it is. For me, to live is You!'"

As I turned to leave, I knew I had prayed a foundational prayer. Much recovery and rebuilding lay before me, but beneath me was the only firm foundation on which to build—Jesus Christ.

Has a loved one's death or the fear of your own death tested your foundation? Let Paul's words, written in the face of death, and Jesus' words to Mary encourage you to offer a foundational prayer of your own. Then begin to rebuild on the risen Christ!

～～

PRAYER IS THE SOIL
IN WHICH HOPE AND HEALING GROW BEST.

Rejoice in the Lord always. I will say it again: Rejoice! Let your gentleness be evident to all. The Lord is near. Do not be anxious about anything, but in everything, by prayer and petition, with thanksgiving, present your requests to God. And the peace of God, which transcends all understanding, will guard your hearts and your minds in Christ Jesus.

Finally, brothers, whatever is true, whatever is noble, whatever is right, whatever is pure, whatever is lovely, whatever is admirable—if anything is excellent or praiseworthy—think about such things. Whatever you have learned or received or heard from me, or seen in me—put it into practice. And the God of peace will be with you.

I rejoice greatly in the Lord that at last you have renewed your concern for me. Indeed, you have been concerned, but you had no opportunity to show it. I am not saying this because I am in need, for I have learned to be content whatever the circumstances. I know what it is to be in need, and I know what it is to have plenty. I have learned the secret of being content in any and every situation, whether well fed or hungry, whether living in plenty or in want. I can do everything through him who gives me strength.

PHILIPPIANS 4:4–13

everal years ago I moved to England, but I have traveled back to the United States many times, often staying with the same families. One family lived in a farmhouse where a tiny upstairs room always awaited me.

I will never forget one visit when, as usual, I lugged my suitcase up the familiar stairs. This time, however, a secret burden on my heart felt heavier than my luggage. As I neared the top of the steps, I saw an old plaque that I had forgotten. It read:

Have You Prayed About It?

Panting physically and spiritually, I had to admit, "No, I haven't!" So I slipped to my knees and finally talked to God about the problem.

Instead of being anxious for nothing, I had become anxious about everything. Instead of praying about everything, I had prayed about nothing. But now, through prayer, my heavy load of worry became God's, and His lightweight gift of peace became mine.

In his book *Tyranny of the Urgent*, Charles Hummel writes that if we are prayerless, "We are saying, with our actions if not our lips, that we do not need God." The deciding factor on how we carry our burdens lies in our answer to the question on that old-fashioned plaque: Have you prayed about it?

~~~

A PRAYERLESS CHRISTIAN IS A POWERLESS CHRISTIAN.

"Do not judge, and you will not be judged. Do not condemn, and you will not be condemned. Forgive, and you will be forgiven. Give, and it will be given to you. A good measure, pressed down, shaken together and running over, will be poured into your lap. For with the measure you use, it will be measured to you."

He also told them this parable: "Can a blind man lead a blind man? Will they not both fall into a pit? A student is not above his teacher, but everyone who is fully trained will be like his teacher.

"Why do you look at the speck of sawdust in your brother's eye and pay no attention to the plank in your own eye? How can you say to your brother, 'Brother, let me take the speck out of your eye,' when you yourself fail to see the plank in your own eye? You hypocrite, first take the plank out of your eye, and then you will see clearly to remove the speck from your brother's eye.

"No good tree bears bad fruit, nor does a bad tree bear good fruit. Each tree is recognized by its own fruit. People do not pick figs from thorn bushes, or grapes from briers. The good man brings good things out of the good stored up in his heart, and the evil man brings evil things out of the evil stored up in his heart. For out of the overflow of his heart his mouth speaks.

LUKE 6:37–45

*S*ome people make judging others their specialty. According to some century-old church records, a congregation in a small Midwestern town in the United States appointed two officers in the church and gave them the titles of "Pointer" and "Beaner." They each had a special responsibility during the Sunday sermons.

The duty of Pointer was to call out the names of those in the congregation who needed to take particular note of the sermon. Beaner's task was to sit in the choir loft with a bean shooter (no doubt the envy of young boys) and awaken drowsy attendees with a well-aimed bean. Who would want to attend that church?

Jesus warned about the danger of pointing out the faults of others. He said people with planks in their eyes should not attempt to remove specks out of other people's eyes. He challenged His hearers to choose humility rather than hypocrisy by always applying the truth to themselves before noting the faults in others.

What would people find in our churches today? Those who specialize in speck removal or plank removal? If it's the latter, they'll likely hear someone say, "I'm glad I heard today's sermon—I really needed it!" And they may want to return next Sunday.

～～

BE PATIENT WITH THE FAULTS OF OTHERS;
THEY HAVE TO BE PATIENT WITH YOURS.

It is written: "I believed; therefore I have spoken." With that same spirit of faith we also believe and therefore speak, because we know that the one who raised the Lord Jesus from the dead will also raise us with Jesus and present us with you in his presence. All this is for your benefit, so that the grace that is reaching more and more people may cause thanksgiving to overflow to the glory of God.

Therefore we do not lose heart. Though outwardly we are wasting away, yet inwardly we are being renewed day by day. For our light and momentary troubles are achieving for us an eternal glory that far outweighs them all. So we fix our eyes not on what is seen, but on what is unseen. For what is seen is temporary, but what is unseen is eternal.

2 CORINTHIANS 4:13–18

Whenever I go to the beauty salon, I must be prepared, oddly enough, to look anything but beautiful—at least to start with.

Sitting beneath an unflattering waterproof cape, I permit someone to work on my straggly hair. As it gets drastically cut, soaked with smelly solution, wrapped around tiny curlers, and then encased in a piece of plastic until it "takes," I steal a glance in the mirror. Horrified, I invariably ask myself, "Why am I paying someone to do this to me?" The satisfying answer is always the same: I hope to walk out of there looking fantastic.

That's the way it is in our Christian walk. This world is God's workshop, where He skillfully changes our lives through trials of faith to make us more like Christ. At times we are horrified at how we look and feel. Paul, urging us not to lose heart, called our trials "light and momentary" (2 Corinthians 4:17). Our trials are achieving for us an eternal glory that will far outweigh them all.

This "hope of glory" is what gives us assurance while God is still working on us. One day, when we exit this world and see Christ face to face, we will be like Him and reflect His beauty.

~~~

PLEASE BE PATIENT—GOD ISN'T FINISHED WITH ME YET.

But thanks be to God, who always leads us in triumphal procession in Christ and through us spreads everywhere the fragrance of the knowledge of him. For we are to God the aroma of Christ among those who are being saved and those who are perishing. To the one we are the smell of death; to the other, the fragrance of life. And who is equal to such a task? Unlike so many, we do not peddle the word of God for profit. On the contrary, in Christ we speak before God with sincerity, like men sent from God.

Are we beginning to commend ourselves again? Or do we need, like some people, letters of recommendation to you or from you? You yourselves are our letter, written on our hearts, known and read by everybody. You show that you are a letter from Christ, the result of our ministry, written not with ink but with the Spirit of the living God, not on tablets of stone but on tablets of human hearts.

Such confidence as this is ours through Christ before God. Not that we are competent in ourselves to claim anything for ourselves, but our competence comes from God. He has made us competent as ministers of a new covenant—not of the letter but of the Spirit; for the letter kills, but the Spirit gives life.

2 CORINTHIANS 2:14-3:6

ost of us can think of someone—perhaps a relative or a friend—who is known for a particular perfume she wears. Even without seeing her, we know when she's nearby. Wordlessly, her fragrance welcomes us into her company.

Every Christian should also be known for wearing a particular perfume—the fragrance of Christ. But it can't be bought at a cosmetic counter. It can't even be bottled and sold by the church. This mysterious perfume rises always and only out of our inner communion with Christ and wafts a subtle yet noticeable influence toward others.

Someone said about a Christian in his small town, "That man never crosses my pathway without me being better for it!" Another remarked of him, "You need only shake his hand to know that he is full of God." Most likely, this admired believer had given a verbal witness at some point. But without the perfume of Christ, his witness would not have been empowered by the Spirit (2 Corinthians 3:6).

The apostle Paul asked, "Who is equal to such a task?" (2:16). The answer is plain: Our fragrance, our entire sufficiency, is from Christ alone, not from ourselves. What fragrance will you be wearing today?

~~~

IF YOU WALK WITH CHRIST,
OTHERS WILL SENSE HIS PRESENCE WITH YOU.

The LORD abhors dishonest scales,
  but accurate weights are his delight.
When pride comes, then comes disgrace,
  but with humility comes wisdom.
The integrity of the upright guides them,
  but the unfaithful are destroyed by their duplicity.
Wealth is worthless in the day of wrath,
  but righteousness delivers from death.
The righteousness of the blameless makes a straight way for them,
  but the wicked are brought down by their own wickedness.
The righteousness of the upright delivers them,
  but the unfaithful are trapped by evil desires.

PROVERBS 11:1-6

I'll always remember the day when as a child I found two coins on the school playground. I brought them home, thinking they wouldn't be missed. But Mother made me take them to my teacher. "They belong to someone else," Mother told me. Since then, God has often reminded me of this early lesson in honesty.

For example, recently as I was putting bags of groceries in my car, I discovered at the bottom of the cart a greeting card I hadn't paid for. I marched back to the cash register, waited in line, apologized for the oversight, and paid for the card. A man behind me, looking dumbfounded, challenged me, "It's only a greeting card! Who would have known? Weren't you a bit silly to come back?"

For a split second I did feel silly. But then these words came to mind: "Should you ever lose your wallet," I replied smiling, "I think you'll hope that somebody silly like me finds it!"

Proverbs 11 reminds us that the Lord delights in honesty (v. 1) and blesses those who do what is right (v. 6). So even though we may give up what seems like some easy money, we gain God's approval. That's worth far more than all the riches in the world. Honesty really does pay!

HONESTY'S REWARD IS SOMETHING
MONEY CANNOT BUY—
A CLEAR CONSCIENCE BEFORE GOD.

At that time Jesus said, "I praise you, Father, Lord of heaven and earth, because you have hidden these things from the wise and learned, and revealed them to little children. Yes, Father, for this was your good pleasure.

"All things have been committed to me by my Father. No one knows the Son except the Father, and no one knows the Father except the Son and those to whom the Son chooses to reveal him.

"Come to me, all you who are weary and burdened, and I will give you rest. Take my yoke upon you and learn from me, for I am gentle and humble in heart, and you will find rest for your souls. For my yoke is easy and my burden is light."

MATTHEW 11:25–30

ou might have heard someone say, "I wrote the book *Humility and How I Achieved It.*" Most people, however, would not seriously mention the word *humility* and their own name in the same sentence. We know that the moment we lay claim to humility it eludes us—rather like this "confession" that appeared in the magazine *Village Voice*: "I felt like a fraud. So I took a full-page ad in the newspaper and confessed to the world that I was a fraud!"

I read the ad and I thought, *A fraud is pretending to be honest.*

Humility without pretending—is it possible? Micah 6:8 provides a vital clue. Micah didn't say, "Be humble," or "Walk humbly." He said, "Walk humbly with your God." His advice pointed to the need for faithful dependence on God and looked ahead to our Lord's words, "Take My yoke upon you and learn from me, for I am gentle and humble in heart" (Matthew 11:29).

Jesus demonstrated humility by walking in total dependence on His Father (John 5:19, 30; 8:28) and by serving others (Matthew 20:28). Only as we take up His yoke and walk humbly with the Father will we learn true humility.

Are we humbly depending on God—or just pretending to be humble?

~~~

TO LEARN TO WALK HUMBLY,
START OUT ON YOUR KNEES.

We have sinned, even as our fathers did;
    we have done wrong and acted wickedly.
When our fathers were in Egypt,
    they gave no thought to your miracles;
they did not remember your many kindnesses,
    and they rebelled by the sea, the Red Sea.
Yet he saved them for his name's sake,
    to make his mighty power known.
He rebuked the Red Sea, and it dried up;
    he led them through the depths as through a desert.
He saved them from the hand of the foe;
    from the hand of the enemy he redeemed them.
The waters covered their adversaries;
    not one of them survived.
Then they believed his promises
    and sang his praise.
But they soon forgot what he had done
    and did not wait for his counsel.
In the desert they gave in to their craving;
    in the wasteland they put God to the test.
So he gave them what they asked for,
    but sent a wasting disease upon them.

PSALM 106:6–15

*S*ome people pray only in a crisis. Their "quick fix" mentality sees God mainly as a problem solver. When merciful solutions come, He is courteously thanked, then more or less forgotten until the next crisis.

The story is told of a little rich girl, accustomed to servants, who was afraid to climb a dark stairway alone. Her mother suggested that she overcome her fear by asking Jesus to go with her up the stairs. When the child reached the top, she was overheard saying, "Thank You, Jesus. You may go now."

We smile, but Psalm 106 contains a serious warning against dismissing God from our lives—as if that were possible. Israel had a tendency to take the Lord's mercies for granted, and God called that rebellion (v. 7). They ended up with malnourished souls because they chose to ignore Him (vv. 13–15). What lessons for us!

Anticipate great things from God, but don't expect Him to come at your beck and call. Instead, be at His beck and call, eager to fulfill His will.

Like the little rich girl, let's ask God to accompany us through life's dark passageways. But instead of dismissing Him when our special needs are met, let's cling to Him as if our lives depended on it. They do!

~~

DO YOU PRAY FOR WHAT YOU WANT,
OR FOR WHAT GOD WANTS?

Jacob left Beersheba and set out for Haran. When he reached a certain place, he stopped for the night because the sun had set. Taking one of the stones there, he put it under his head and lay down to sleep. He had a dream in which he saw a stairway resting on the earth, with its top reaching to heaven, and the angels of God were ascending and descending on it. There above it stood the LORD, and he said: "I am the LORD, the God of your father Abraham and the God of Isaac. I will give you and your descendants the land on which you are lying. Your descendants will be like the dust of the earth, and you will spread out to the west and to the east, to the north and to the south. All peoples on earth will be blessed through you and your offspring. I am with you and will watch over you wherever you go, and I will bring you back to this land. I will not leave you until I have done what I have promised you."

When Jacob awoke from his sleep, he thought, "Surely the LORD is in this place, and I was not aware of it." He was afraid and said, "How awesome is this place! This is none other than the house of God; this is the gate of heaven."

GENESIS 28:10–17

One afternoon I was deeply engrossed in a book. With the radio and TV off, the entire house seemed quiet. Suddenly my surroundings went dead, as if something alive had departed. And it had—the electricity had gone off! I had forgotten that some electrical appliances emit a barely audible hum. I had grown so accustomed to it that I had lost my awareness of it.

The Lord used that incident to expose one of my spiritual problems. I had grown so accustomed to His abiding presence that I was taking for granted the dynamic difference He was making in my life. That painful revelation of my spiritual need also became its cure, and I was able to exclaim with Jacob, "Surely the LORD is in this place, and I was not aware of it" (Genesis 28:16). But I do now!

Commenting on Jacob's lack of awareness, pastor and author A. W. Tozer wrote, "That was his trouble, and it is ours. Men do not know that God is here. What a difference it would make if they knew!"

Has your spiritual awareness been dulled because you've taken God's presence for granted? May it be so enlivened today that you too can exclaim, "The Lord is here—and I know it!"

GOD'S PRESENCE WITH US
IS HIS GREATEST PRESENT TO US.

[Jesus] said to them, "Why are you troubled, and why do doubts rise in your minds? Look at my hands and my feet. It is I myself! Touch me and see; a ghost does not have flesh and bones, as you see I have."

When he had said this, he showed them his hands and feet. And while they still did not believe it because of joy and amazement, he asked them, "Do you have anything here to eat?" They gave him a piece of broiled fish, and he took it and ate it in their presence.

He said to them, "This is what I told you while I was still with you: Everything must be fulfilled that is written about me in the Law of Moses, the Prophets and the Psalms."

Then he opened their minds so they could understand the Scriptures. He told them, "This is what is written: The Christ will suffer and rise from the dead on the third day, and repentance and forgiveness of sins will be preached in his name to all nations, beginning at Jerusalem. You are witnesses of these things."

LUKE 24:38-48

I was seventeen when I first examined the gospel. Not that I felt I needed to, mind you. I was a churchgoer, a do-gooder, and above all I was sincere. But I had met some Christian teenagers who had something I didn't have, and I was curious.

Two things troubled me. First was their stress on sin and repentance. I had always compared myself favorably with those I considered to be mega-sinners—murderers, gangsters, and the like—making me feel more grateful than sinful.

A second thing that bothered me about these Christians was their insistence that Jesus had to die and rise again. *Well, He didn't need to go to such extremes for me*, I thought.

Then one evening God prompted me to compare myself with Him. I realized my sinfulness, and I eagerly repented! At last I appreciated the necessity of Christ's death and resurrection. If sin's penalty didn't fall on us, where else could it fall? Calvary was the only place. In His immeasurable love, Jesus did what was necessary (Luke 24:46). Dying, He allowed sin's penalty to fall on Him. Rising, He became our living Savior to overcome sin's power in us.

You don't have to take my word for it, of course. But have you taken His?

~~~

IF YOU SAY, "I'M NO WORSE THAN THE REST,"
YOU STILL FAIL GOD'S TEST.

Now Ahab told Jezebel everything Elijah had done and how he had killed all the prophets with the sword. So Jezebel sent a messenger to Elijah to say, "May the gods deal with me, be it ever so severely, if by this time tomorrow I do not make your life like that of one of them."

Elijah was afraid and ran for his life. When he came to Beersheba in Judah, he left his servant there, while he himself went a day's journey into the desert. He came to a broom tree, sat down under it and prayed that he might die. "I have had enough, LORD," he said. "Take my life; I am no better than my ancestors." Then he lay down under the tree and fell asleep.

All at once an angel touched him and said, "Get up and eat." He looked around, and there by his head was a cake of bread baked over hot coals, and a jar of water. He ate and drank and then lay down again.

The angel of the LORD came back a second time and touched him and said, "Get up and eat, for the journey is too much for you." So he got up and ate and drank. Strengthened by that food, he traveled for forty days and forty nights until he reached Horeb, the mountain of God. There he went into a cave and spent the night.

1 KINGS 19:1–9

Our children grew up accustomed to thanking God for their food and asking Him to bless it. Once, after my husband had prayed, Tina asked, "Daddy, why did you ask God to bless this food to our wobbly knees?"

He had said "bodily needs," not "wobbly knees." Tina's misunderstanding not only reminded us of the necessity of food, but it also encouraged us to ask God for strength when we face life's stresses.

In today's reading, we find Elijah in a "wobbly" condition. After his mountaintop experience in 1 Kings 18, he ended up in the wilderness—tired, discouraged, and hungry. An angel brought him food, and later God Himself ministered to Elijah's discouragement by speaking to him in a still, small voice.

Like Elijah, everyone has "wobbly" moments. If we haven't taken time to care for our physical needs, we need to rest and eat. And if we are feeling weak spiritually, we must take time to be quiet and listen to the still, small voice of God in His Word. This is essential food for our souls.

It's good to pause at mealtime to ask God to use the food to meet our bodily needs. It's even more crucial to read His Word and ask Him to nourish us spiritually. After all, He alone is the One who can strengthen "wobbly knees."

～～～

WHEN LIFE GETS YOU DOWN, TAKE TIME TO LOOK UP.

Brothers, think of what you were when you were called. Not many of you were wise by human standards; not many were influential; not many were of noble birth. But God chose the foolish things of the world to shame the wise; God chose the weak things of the world to shame the strong. He chose the lowly things of this world and the despised things—and the things that are not—to nullify the things that are, so that no one may boast before him. It is because of him that you are in Christ Jesus, who has become for us wisdom from God—that is, our righteousness, holiness and redemption. Therefore, as it is written: "Let him who boasts boast in the Lord."

1 CORINTHIANS 1:26–31

*I*f we are committed to pleasing Christ, we will try to have a good testimony among unbelievers. Some Christians assume that being a good example means keeping up an appearance of strength—even when they are weak. They have the misconception that any appearance of weakness hinders their testimony. Thus begins a subtle slide to spiritual play-acting, or what I call "the big cover-up."

When seeking to have a good testimony, we must ask whether we are trying to represent God or ourselves. And when seeking to be strong, we must ask, "In whose strength—God's or ours?"

According to Paul, the Lord enables us to testify of Him and His strength, not by despising our weakness but by using it, "that no one may boast before him" (1 Corinthians 1:29).

Are unbelievers best won to Christ by "strong" people who pretend they're never weak, or by "weak" people who testify of a strength not their own? Unbelievers often say of the former, "I could never be like that." But of the "weak" people, they more often say, "If Christ can help them, perhaps He has something for me."

Let's honestly admit our weakness and offer it to God for His use.

~~~

TO SHOW OTHERS WHAT CHRIST WILL DO FOR THEM,
SHOW THEM WHAT CHRIST HAS DONE FOR YOU.

Trust in the LORD with all your heart
and lean not on your own understanding;
in all your ways acknowledge him,
and he will make your paths straight.
Do not be wise in your own eyes;
fear the LORD and shun evil.
This will bring health to your body
and nourishment to your bones.
Honor the LORD with your wealth,
with the firstfruits of all your crops;
then your barns will be filled to overflowing,
and your vats will brim over with new wine.
My son, do not despise the LORD's discipline
and do not resent his rebuke,
because the LORD disciplines those he loves,
as a father the son he delights in.

PROVERBS 3:5-12

Solomon warned us not to lean on our own understanding (Proverbs 3:5). That implies we are prone to make mistakes in judgment. And how we hate having our mistakes corrected!

Some people detest correction so much that their main goal in life seems to be attempting to avoid or hide all their mistakes. But let's be practical. Correction, if well received, can save us a lot of grief.

Eugene Peterson tells about a personal experience that illustrates the value of correction. With his lawn mower tipped on its side, Eugene struggled to remove the blade so he could sharpen it. When his biggest wrench wouldn't budge the nut, he slipped a four-foot length of pipe over the wrench handle for more leverage. When that failed, he started banging on the pipe with a huge rock. Finally his neighbor pointed out that the threads on the bolt went the other way. When Eugene reversed his exertions, the nut turned easily. He said, "I was saved from frustration and failure."

Are you forcing your life in the wrong direction? Welcome the correction of your heavenly Father, who delights in you. Trust His wisdom instead of your own, and He will redirect your life. That's a promise! (Proverbs 3:6).

～

THE ONLY WAY TO BE RIGHT IS TO AGREE WITH GOD WHEN HE SAYS WE'RE WRONG.

The senseless man does not know,
    fools do not understand,
that though the wicked spring up like grass
    and all evildoers flourish,
they will be forever destroyed.
But you, O LORD, are exalted forever.
For surely your enemies, O LORD,
    surely your enemies will perish;
    all evildoers will be scattered.
You have exalted my horn like that of a wild ox;
    fine oils have been poured upon me.
My eyes have seen the defeat of my adversaries;
    my ears have heard the rout of my wicked foes.
The righteous will flourish like a palm tree,
    they will grow like a cedar of Lebanon;
planted in the house of the LORD,
    they will flourish in the courts of our God.
They will still bear fruit in old age,
    they will stay fresh and green,
proclaiming, "The LORD is upright;
    he is my Rock, and there is no wickedness in him."

PSALM 92:6–15

*I*n her book *Less Stress, More Peace*, Verna Birkey refers to a seventy-two-year-old woman named Jo who worried about growing older. Jo called these fears "ugly gremlins." To gain victory over them, she wrote a "Declaration of Commitment and Faith," which I quote in part:

"My dear heavenly Father, how can I ever express how grateful I am for Your great care over me through the years? You have been so good. Why then, Lord, do these ugly gremlins come into my thinking? I worry about losing this wonderful husband that You have given me. Will I have to suffer a long illness before You take me home? What if I end up in a rest home? What if I become senile?

"There now, I've verbalized them! Those ugly gremlins! Lord, I now commit all these worries about old age to You. I will claim the promise You have given me in Psalm 92, that I shall still bring forth fruit in my old age. Each time one of these fears comes up, I will go back and review this commitment until I have peace. I can trust You with my old age. I praise You, Lord!"

Why not write your own "Declaration of Commitment and Faith" concerning your "ugly gremlins"?

WORRY IS FUTILE; FAITH IS FRUITFUL.

They went to a place called Gethsemane, and Jesus said to his disciples, "Sit here while I pray." He took Peter, James and John along with him, and he began to be deeply distressed and troubled. "My soul is overwhelmed with sorrow to the point of death," he said to them. "Stay here and keep watch."

Going a little farther, he fell to the ground and prayed that if possible the hour might pass from him. "Abba, Father," he said, "everything is possible for you. Take this cup from me. Yet not what I will, but what you will."

Then he returned to his disciples and found them sleeping. "Simon," he said to Peter, "are you asleep? Could you not keep watch for one hour? Watch and pray so that you will not fall into temptation. The spirit is willing, but the body is weak."

Once more he went away and prayed the same thing. When he came back, he again found them sleeping, because their eyes were heavy. They did not know what to say to him.

Returning the third time, he said to them, "Are you still sleeping and resting? Enough! The hour has come. Look, the Son of Man is betrayed into the hands of sinners. Rise! Let us go! Here comes my betrayer!"

MARK 14:32–42

In today's society, two popular factors, the "feel-good factor" and the "look-good factor," are being confused with success. Anyone not feeling or looking good is often regarded as mediocre—even a failure.

The church can easily fall into this trap, all in the name of longing to have a good testimony for the Lord. A deeper look at Christ's own testimony will set us straight.

In Mark 14:32–42, Jesus was nearing His atoning death at Calvary. As Jesus fought and won the battle of the will, Luke said that "His sweat was like drops of blood" (22:44). In all this and the terrible agony of the crucifixion that followed, Jesus neither felt good nor looked good. Rather, He was good and did good by choosing His Father's will and fulfilling it. His anguished obedience was later followed by joyful resurrection.

Has your heavenly Father entrusted you with an agonizing situation in which it's unrealistic to feel good or look good? Don't despair! He values what you are and what you do as you die to self and embrace His will. Jesus knows that this often feels and looks messy. The truth is, it honors God and eventually leads to victory and joy. What greater testimony than this?

～

GOD BRINGS BEAUTY OUT OF UGLY SITUATIONS.

But in fact God has arranged the parts in the body, every one of them, just as he wanted them to be. If they were all one part, where would the body be? As it is, there are many parts, but one body.

The eye cannot say to the hand, "I don't need you!" And the head cannot say to the feet, "I don't need you!" On the contrary, those parts of the body that seem to be weaker are indispensable, and the parts that we think are less honorable we treat with special honor. And the parts that are unpresentable are treated with special modesty, while our presentable parts need no special treatment. But God has combined the members of the body and has given greater honor to the parts that lacked it, so that there should be no division in the body, but that its parts should have equal concern for each other. If one part suffers, every part suffers with it; if one part is honored, every part rejoices with it.

Now you are the body of Christ, and each one of you is a part of it.

1 CORINTHIANS 12:18–27

Twice in my life I've broken one of my little toes by colliding with furniture. Ouch! For days I limped painfully, my body protecting its tiny injured member. My body was doing exactly what it was designed to do. It supported and sympathized with the part of me that was hurting. Gradually my toe healed, resuming its thankless task.

Although I'll never again take my toes for granted, I sometimes take for granted certain members of the church. Paul taught that the church is the body of Christ (1 Corinthians 12:12–27), not merely like the body of Christ. Each member has God-given abilities to support and sympathize with other members.

If Christ's church is to function the way God designed it, there are three things we dare not do: refuse to fellowship with others; let fear and lack of love cause us to withhold our gifts from others; disregard or oppose the gifts of others through pride and envy.

Instead, we need to be actively using our spiritual gifts to the benefit of fellow members of Christ's body. Only when we experience both the giving and receiving of Christ's healing love for broken members will we be ready to reach out to a broken world.

~~~

A HEALTHY CHURCH IS THE BEST WITNESS
TO A HURTING WORLD.

As soon as they left the synagogue, they went with James and John to the home of Simon and Andrew. Simon's mother-in-law was in bed with a fever, and they told Jesus about her. So he went to her, took her hand and helped her up. The fever left her and she began to wait on them.

That evening after sunset the people brought to Jesus all the sick and demon-possessed. The whole town gathered at the door, and Jesus healed many who had various diseases. He also drove out many demons, but he would not let the demons speak because they knew who he was. Very early in the morning, while it was still dark, Jesus got up, left the house and went off to a solitary place, where he prayed. Simon and his companions went to look for him, and when they found him, they exclaimed: "Everyone is looking for you!"

Jesus replied, "Let us go somewhere else—to the nearby villages— so I can preach there also. That is why I have come." So he traveled throughout Galilee, preaching in their synagogues and driving out demons.

MARK 1:29–39

*N*o one is indispensable! Most of us readily agree with that statement but live as if we don't believe it. We complain, "I simply can't do it all!" yet keep right on trying to do it all.

Mark, one of the gospel writers, described Jesus as He faced many demands on His time. He launched His ministry, called and trained disciples, taught and preached, healed and liberated, ministered to individuals and crowds.

How did He do it all? His priorities determined His use of time. He withdrew regularly to get time alone with His Father for rest and prayer. He was with His Father when His disciples intruded to say, "Everyone is looking for you" (Mark 1:37). But Jesus replied, "Let us go somewhere else—to the nearby villages—so I can preach there also " (v. 38).

Whenever Jesus turned His face toward one responsibility, He had to turn His back on another, just as we must do. But instead of letting the pressure of unmet needs determine His direction, He responded according to His sense of God's purpose. He sharpened that sense daily through solitude with His Father—and so should we.

Get your priorities from the Lord, and you won't be frustrated when you find you can't do it all.

~~

WHEN YOU DON'T KNOW WHAT TO DO FIRST,
GIVE THE LORD FIRST PLACE.

Therefore, my brothers, you whom I love and long for, my joy and crown, that is how you should stand firm in the Lord, dear friends!

I plead with Euodia and I plead with Syntyche to agree with each other in the Lord. Yes, and I ask you, loyal yokefellow, help these women who have contended at my side in the cause of the gospel, along with Clement and the rest of my fellow workers, whose names are in the book of life.

Rejoice in the Lord always. I will say it again: Rejoice! Let your gentleness be evident to all. The Lord is near. Do not be anxious about anything, but in everything, by prayer and petition, with thanksgiving, present your requests to God. And the peace of God, which transcends all understanding, will guard your hearts and your minds in Christ Jesus.

Finally, brothers, whatever is true, whatever is noble, whatever is right, whatever is pure, whatever is lovely, whatever is admirable—if anything is excellent or praiseworthy—think about such things. Whatever you have learned or received or heard from me, or seen in me—put it into practice. And the God of peace will be with you.

PHILIPPIANS 4:1–9

*L*et me introduce two amazing people to you: Miracle Man Jim and Weak Flea Kathryn—as they cheerfully call themselves.

In spite of Jim's battle with cancer and Kathryn's pain from the effects of childhood polio, their letters are sprinkled with the words *exciting, marvelous, innumerable blessings, golden opportunities, peace, joy*. "We celebrate something every day," Kathryn recently wrote.

Jim and Kathryn are illustrations of a poster I once saw that bore an exquisite rose with the caption: "Some people complain that roses have thorns; others rejoice that thorns have roses."

The apostle Paul's letter to the struggling group of believers in Philippi was written while he was imprisoned in Rome. Yet he was able to encourage them to "rejoice in the Lord always" (Philippians 4:4) and to meditate on what is true, noble, right, pure, lovely, admirable, excellent, and praiseworthy (v. 8). Paul didn't tell them to deny their worries but to give them to God through prayer and petition (v. 6).

We all need to become avid rose gardeners—hunting for buds of beauty within our thorny circumstances. It's a sure cure for complaining.

~~

RATHER THAN COMPLAIN ABOUT THE THORNS ON ROSES, BE THANKFUL FOR THE ROSES AMONG THORNS.

This is how we know what love is: Jesus Christ laid down his life for us. And we ought to lay down our lives for our brothers. If anyone has material possessions and sees his brother in need but has no pity on him, how can the love of God be in him? Dear children, let us not love with words or tongue but with actions and in truth. This then is how we know that we belong to the truth, and how we set our hearts at rest in his presence whenever our hearts condemn us. For God is greater than our hearts, and he knows everything.

Dear friends, if our hearts do not condemn us, we have confidence before God and receive from him anything we ask, because we obey his commands and do what pleases him. And this is his command: to believe in the name of his Son, Jesus Christ, and to love one another as he commanded us. Those who obey his commands live in him, and he in them. And this is how we know that he lives in us: We know it by the Spirit he gave us.

1 JOHN 3:16–24

A young man sent a love letter to his girlfriend. It read: "Darling, I'd climb the highest mountain, sail the widest ocean, cross the hottest desert just to see you. P.S.—I'll be over Saturday night if it doesn't rain."

We chuckle at his fickleness but feel bad for the girl who, like all of us, longs for love in action, not empty promises.

John said that Jesus Christ showed us what true love is when "[He] laid down His life for us." But John continued, "We ought to lay down our lives for our brothers" (1 John 3:16).

The Greek word used for love in 1 John 3:16 is *agape*. This kind of love is characterized by sacrifice. It is a love based on the will, not on emotions. It's not a feeling subject to the whims of our convenience. It is a decision to love another despite the cost.

Laying down our lives for others usually doesn't mean dying. Often it costs little more than stopping what we're doing and entering someone's world of need. I once felt prompted by the Holy Spirit to stop scrubbing my kitchen floor to visit a neighbor. She later accepted Christ, in part due to the friendship we had established during that visit.

Don't miss small opportunities to love by waiting for big ones. With agape love, even small acts of love are big.

~~

LOVE IN DEED IS LOVE INDEED!

What good is it, my brothers, if a man claims to have faith but has no deeds? Can such faith save him? Suppose a brother or sister is without clothes and daily food. If one of you says to him, "Go, I wish you well; keep warm and well fed," but does nothing about his physical needs, what good is it? In the same way, faith by itself, if it is not accompanied by action, is dead.

But someone will say, "You have faith; I have deeds."

Show me your faith without deeds, and I will show you my faith by what I do. You believe that there is one God. Good! Even the demons believe that—and shudder.

You foolish man, do you want evidence that faith without deeds is useless? Was not our ancestor Abraham considered righteous for what he did when he offered his son Isaac on the altar? You see that his faith and his actions were working together, and his faith was made complete by what he did. And the scripture was fulfilled that says, "Abraham believed God, and it was credited to him as righteousness," and he was called God's friend. You see that a person is justified by what he does and not by faith alone.

JAMES 2:14–24

*M*ary is a senior citizen with many health problems. She is also a widow with a home to keep up. No use expecting Mary to do much in the church or community anymore, right? Wrong! In spite of her limitations, her faith continues to work.

Although Mary and her late husband had no children, they had a ministry to other people's children. Now alone, she coordinates a new ministry in her church for women who might be considering abortion.

Mary writes, "If we are preaching against abortion, we should offer pregnant women our help. Within two days I've had four volunteers to help me. Now we must meet to set up a plan of action."

A plan of action—how typical of a working faith! How different from people who see a desperate need and moan, "Why doesn't somebody do something?" but are unwilling to be that somebody!

In James 2 we read that Abraham obediently offered his son Isaac on the altar. This act is cited as a work that proved the reality of his faith (vv. 21–23).

Mary, like Abraham, has a faith that works. Our needy world could use many more like them. How can you put your faith into action today?

~~

FAITH NEVER STANDS AROUND
WITH ITS HANDS IN ITS POCKETS.

Lord, you have been our dwelling place
    throughout all generations.
Before the mountains were born
    or you brought forth the earth and the world,
    from everlasting to everlasting you are God.
You turn men back to dust,
    saying, "Return to dust, O sons of men."
For a thousand years in your sight
    are like a day that has just gone by,
    or like a watch in the night . . . .
Teach us to number our days aright,
    that we may gain a heart of wisdom.

PSALM 90:1-4, 12

When we are young, we tend to live as if we think we'll never die. Yet the psalmist said that if we want to gain a heart of wisdom, we need to start numbering our days, whatever our age (90:12). The best way to number them is to make sure that our life is patterned each day after the example of Jesus. Only then can we anticipate that our life will not have been lived in vain.

James Dobson, a well-known authority on the family, tells a story about his father, who was greatly loved by all who knew him. James Dobson, Sr., spent much time in intercessory prayer, considering prayer for others his most important business on earth. In fact, he specified in his will that only two words were to be put on his tombstone following his name: He Prayed.

Of the thousands of verbs in our language, by which one are you likely to be remembered? He served. She cared. He supported. She praised. What if dishonoring verbs are linked with you because of thoughtlessness or selfishness? He cheated. She complained. It's not too late to repent and trade those descriptions in for Christ-honoring ones. Then trust God to build them into your character. That's the best way to number your days!

~~~

LIVING FOR THE LORD LEAVES A LASTING LEGACY.

Therefore, rid yourselves of all malice and all deceit, hypocrisy, envy, and slander of every kind. Like newborn babies, crave pure spiritual milk, so that by it you may grow up in your salvation, now that you have tasted that the Lord is good.

As you come to him, the living Stone—rejected by men but chosen by God and precious to him—you also, like living stones, are being built into a spiritual house to be a holy priesthood, offering spiritual sacrifices acceptable to God through Jesus Christ.

1 PETER 2:1-5

*W*henever children visit relatives, they often hear this kind of greeting: "My, haven't you grown!" This embarrasses them, but inside they're glad they've outgrown babyhood. Not that babyhood is bad. How else can life begin? But it is sad when babies remain babies.

Sometimes mature Christians, eager to keep new converts from stagnating in their growth, make them feel guilty for being babies and rush them down the road to maturity before they are ready.

In 1 Peter 2, the apostle affirmed that spiritual babyhood is normal. Instead of forcing newborns to run before they can walk, he encouraged them to crave the wholesome milk of Christ's basic teaching. He knew that as they continued to take in milk, in time they would move on to solid food and maturity (Hebrews 5:14). What a joy to see that happen!

Several years ago I received a phone call from a friend, a former drug addict and now a Christian. "Hi, Chris," I responded cheerily. "How are you doing?" A long, worrisome pause made me wonder, *Had he slipped back?* Then came words that uplifted my heart: "Growing, Joanie, growing!" That said it all.

I hope you can say the same.

~~

THE CHRISTIAN LIFE IS MORE LIKE
CLIMBING A MOUNTAIN THAN RIDING AN ELEVATOR.

Now the Passover and the Feast of Unleavened Bread were only two days away, and the chief priests and the teachers of the law were looking for some sly way to arrest Jesus and kill him. "But not during the Feast," they said, "or the people may riot."

While he was in Bethany, reclining at the table in the home of a man known as Simon the Leper, a woman came with an alabaster jar of very expensive perfume, made of pure nard. She broke the jar and poured the perfume on his head.

Some of those present were saying indignantly to one another, "Why this waste of perfume? It could have been sold for more than a year's wages and the money given to the poor." And they rebuked her harshly.

"Leave her alone," said Jesus. "Why are you bothering her? She has done a beautiful thing to me. The poor you will always have with you, and you can help them any time you want. But you will not always have me. She did what she could. She poured perfume on my body beforehand to prepare for my burial. I tell you the truth, wherever the gospel is preached throughout the world, what she has done will also be told, in memory of her."

MARK 14:1-9

*I*n today's performance-driven world, Christians are often more critical of their own acts of service than God is. Many seek to honor Him in word and deed yet feel that nothing they do is ever good enough to please Him. The Bible reading in Mark 14 will encourage such distraught servants.

From what we learn in John 12, we know that the woman in Mark 14 was Mary, the one who regarded listening at Jesus' feet as more important than preparing an impressive meal (Luke 10:38–42). F. B. Meyer wrote this about her: "Probably, of all His followers, Mary alone had understood His references to His death, and as she could not be present to perform the last offices of love, she rendered them in advance."

Her loveless critics called her extravagant anointing of Jesus' head with costly oil a waste. But Jesus quickly vindicated her by acknowledging that she had done a good work for Him simply by doing what she could.

Are you frustrated because of what you can't do and critical of what you can? Are the murmurings of others drowning out God's "well done"? Rest for a while at Jesus' feet and gain Mary's understanding. Then rise up and do what you can, knowing that He will be pleased.

~~~

WHEN YOU GIVE YOUR ALL, YOUR LITTLE IS A LOT.

Therefore, my dear friends, as you have always obeyed—not only in my presence, but now much more in my absence—continue to work out your salvation with fear and trembling, for it is God who works in you to will and to act according to his good purpose.

Do everything without complaining or arguing, so that you may become blameless and pure, children of God without fault in a crooked and depraved generation, in which you shine like stars in the universe as you hold out the word of life—in order that I may boast on the day of Christ that I did not run or labor for nothing. But even if I am being poured out like a drink offering on the sacrifice and service coming from your faith, I am glad and rejoice with all of you. So you too should be glad and rejoice with me.

PHILIPPIANS 2:12–18

Each day as your body performs its round of duties, it's not functioning without resources. The fact is, your body is working out what your well-supplied digestive system is working in. It's a physical law, a cooperation between supply and demand, which is fundamental to healthy living.

In his letter to the Philippians, Paul described a spiritual law that is similar. As we faithfully "work out" our salvation, demonstrating the reality of our faith through acts and attitudes of obedience to God's Word, we can't do it in our own energy. We must rely on God, "who works in [us] to will and to act according to his good purpose" (2:13).

Warren Wiersbe tells of a frustrated Sunday school teacher whose class wasn't growing as it should. She wore herself out working harder and harder, yet nothing changed. Finally, after recognizing that her ministry was self-motivated and self-activated, things began to change. "I've learned to draw constantly on the Lord's power," she said, "and things are different!"

This woman still works hard as a teacher, but no longer self-sufficiently. Instead, she's learned to work out, moment by moment, what God works in. Have you?

~~~

YOU CAN TRUST GOD TO DO WHAT YOU CANNOT DO.

So I say, live by the Spirit, and you will not gratify the desires of the sinful nature. For the sinful nature desires what is contrary to the Spirit, and the Spirit what is contrary to the sinful nature. They are in conflict with each other, so that you do not do what you want. But if you are led by the Spirit, you are not under law.

The acts of the sinful nature are obvious: sexual immorality, impurity and debauchery; idolatry and witchcraft; hatred, discord, jealousy, fits of rage, selfish ambition, dissensions, factions and envy; drunkenness, orgies, and the like. I warn you, as I did before, that those who live like this will not inherit the kingdom of God.

But the fruit of the Spirit is love, joy, peace, patience, kindness, goodness, faithfulness, gentleness and self-control. Against such things there is no law. Those who belong to Christ Jesus have crucified the sinful nature with its passions and desires. Since we live by the Spirit, let us keep in step with the Spirit. Let us not become conceited, provoking and envying each other.

GALATIANS 5:16–26

*M*ark was twenty-one and dependent on drugs.

Finding happiness was his big goal in life, a goal that had eluded him. Once, while talking with our family, his frustration erupted: "Look, all I want in life is happiness. I want to feel happy. Is that asking too much?"

Sadly, Mark was asking far too little of life. What he really was seeking but hadn't realized was not happiness but joy. He couldn't accept that real joy is a fruit of something, or Someone, much greater than happiness. He came very close to Jesus Christ—close enough to taste the life that results in the joy he so deeply craved. But eventually he walked away, only to remain unhappy.

According to Bible scholar Ian Barclay, "Happiness is not a biblical word at all. It is derived from the root to happen. Clearly, what happens to us will affect our happiness." Joy, on the other hand, is a fruit of God's Spirit and is not affected by good or bad happenings. Joy is not dependent on our circumstances. It is dependent, as we ourselves need to be, on God Himself who dwells within us.

We should desire to have this joy in our lives, without chasing after it. Let's live and walk in the Spirit so that the fruit of joy will naturally burst forth.

HAPPINESS DEPENDS ON HAPPENINGS;
JOY DEPENDS ON JESUS.

Then the Lord said, "I will surely return to you about this time next year, and Sarah your wife will have a son."

Now Sarah was listening at the entrance to the tent, which was behind him. Abraham and Sarah were already old and well advanced in years, and Sarah was past the age of childbearing. So Sarah laughed to herself as she thought, "After I am worn out and my master is old, will I now have this pleasure?"

Then the Lord said to Abraham, "Why did Sarah laugh and say, 'Will I really have a child, now that I am old?' Is anything too hard for the LORD? I will return to you at the appointed time next year and Sarah will have a son."

Sarah was afraid, so she lied and said, "I did not laugh."

But he said, "Yes, you did laugh."

GENESIS 18:10–15

People have always had a tendency to want to "help" God when He seems slow to fulfill His promises.

The Lord had promised Abraham that his descendants would be as countless as the stars and that an heir would come from his own aging body (Genesis 15:1–5). Abraham believed the Lord, but Sarah ran out of patience. She talked Abraham into fathering children through her maidservant Hagar. Ishmael was born, but he wasn't the son of promise (17:18–21). Fourteen years later, when Abraham and Sarah were very old, God did the impossible—Sarah conceived, and the son of promise, Isaac, was born.

A godly woman shared this story: "Once during my husband's absence, a crisis arose. I needed to act quickly, but I was utterly helpless. Finally I prayed, 'Lord, this is impossible for me. You'll have to take over completely. I can't even help You!'" She testified that God then accomplished the impossible when she admitted her helplessness.

When we depend on ourselves, people see what we can do, and our testimony is, "Didn't I do well!" When we depend on God, people see what He can do, and our testimony is, "Didn't God do well!" Which testimony will you have today?

~~~

FACING AN IMPOSSIBILITY
GIVES US THE OPPORTUNITY TO TRUST GOD.

For the message of the cross is foolishness to those who are perishing, but to us who are being saved it is the power of God. For it is written:

> *"I will destroy the wisdom of the wise;*
> *the intelligence of the intelligent I will frustrate."*

Where is the wise man? Where is the scholar? Where is the philosopher of this age? Has not God made foolish the wisdom of the world? For since in the wisdom of God the world through its wisdom did not know him, God was pleased through the foolishness of what was preached to save those who believe. Jews demand miraculous signs and Greeks look for wisdom, but we preach Christ crucified: a stumbling block to Jews and foolishness to Gentiles, but to those whom God has called, both Jews and Greeks, Christ the power of God and the wisdom of God. For the foolishness of God is wiser than man's wisdom, and the weakness of God is stronger than man's strength.

Brothers, think of what you were when you were called. Not many of you were wise by human standards; not many were influential; not many were of noble birth. But God chose the foolish things of the world to shame the wise; God chose the weak things of the world to shame the strong. He chose the lowly things of this world and the despised things—and the things that are not—to nullify the things that are, so that no one may boast before him.

1 CORINTHIANS 1:18-29

There's a Chinese tale about a young man who captured a tiger cub, brought it home, and raised it in a cage. When it was full grown, the man loved to brag about how ferocious and powerful it was. "That tiger isn't wild anymore," scoffed his friends. "He's as tame as an old house cat." This went on until a wise old man overheard them and said, "There's only one way to know whether this tiger is ferocious or not. Open the cage!"

The young man smiled, placed his hand on the latch, and challenged his friends, "Want to try out my tiger?"

Many people view the gospel of Jesus Christ as a tame and powerless fantasy. Yet in 1 Corinthians 1:18 the apostle Paul called it "the power of God." He used the Greek word *dunamis*, which is the root for our word *dynamite*. Paul said that to an unbeliever the gospel is foolishness, but anyone who is willing to believe it will experience the "dynamite" of God. A tiger's strength, of course, is destructive and can bring death, but the power of the gospel always leads to life and freedom. It destroys guilt and breaks the stranglehold of sinful habits.

If we have experienced this power, let's challenge others to "try out our tiger."

~~~

TO EXPERIENCE GOD'S POWER,
WE MUST FIRST ADMIT THAT WE ARE WEAK.

Praise be to the God and Father of our Lord Jesus Christ! In his great mercy he has given us new birth into a living hope through the resurrection of Jesus Christ from the dead, and into an inheritance that can never perish, spoil or fade—kept in heaven for you, who through faith are shielded by God's power until the coming of the salvation that is ready to be revealed in the last time. In this you greatly rejoice, though now for a little while you may have had to suffer grief in all kinds of trials. These have come so that your faith— of greater worth than gold, which perishes even though refined by fire—may be proved genuine and may result in praise, glory and honor when Jesus Christ is revealed. Though you have not seen him, you love him; and even though you do not see him now, you believe in him and are filled with an inexpressible and glorious joy, for you are receiving the goal of your faith, the salvation of your souls.

1 PETER 1:3–9

A severe trial is sometimes called an "acid test." This term originated during times when gold was widely circulated. Nitric acid was applied to an object of gold to see if it was genuine or not. If it was fake, the acid decomposed it; if it was genuine, the gold was unaffected.

In God's view, our faith is "of greater worth than gold," and it too must be tested (1 Peter 1:7). But these "acid tests" are positive ones. The Lord is working to reveal genuine faith, not to expose false faith.

During hard times, though, we may feel overwhelmed with the fear that our faith is decomposing. Ronald Dunn, a Bible teacher who has experienced much personal tragedy, knows what we are going through. He writes, "I'm often mystified . . . I don't understand why it is that as I endeavor to live for God and pray and believe, everything seems to be falling apart. Sometimes I struggle, and I say, 'Dear Lord, why are You allowing this to happen?'" Dunn concludes, "It's good for us to remember that God is not an arsonist; He's a refiner."

If you're undergoing a test of your faith, you can rejoice because it may be the very thing that God wants to use to purify and strengthen you.

~~

GOD IS NOT AN ARSONIST; HE'S A REFINER.—DUNN

Now we know that if the earthly tent we live in is destroyed, we have a building from God, an eternal house in heaven, not built by human hands. Meanwhile we groan, longing to be clothed with our heavenly dwelling, because when we are clothed, we will not be found naked. For while we are in this tent, we groan and are burdened, because we do not wish to be unclothed but to be clothed with our heavenly dwelling, so that what is mortal may be swallowed up by life. Now it is God who has made us for this very purpose and has given us the Spirit as a deposit, guaranteeing what is to come.

Therefore we are always confident and know that as long as we are at home in the body we are away from the Lord. We live by faith, not by sight. We are confident, I say, and would prefer to be away from the body and at home with the Lord. So we make it our goal to please him, whether we are at home in the body or away from it.

2 CORINTHIANS 5:1–9

My favorite gospel tract is called "When I Think of Heaven." It's written by Joni Eareckson Tada, who is paralyzed from her neck down because of a diving accident that happened during her teenage years. Joni admits that thinking about heaven isn't always easy, especially since we have to die to get there, unless Jesus returns first! Yet God works through trials to help us focus our minds on heaven.

As one who lives, travels, and ministers in a wheelchair, Joni writes confidently about heaven: "There's not a doubt in my mind that I'll be fantastically more excited and ready for it than if I were on my feet. You see, suffering gets us ready for heaven. Heaven becomes our passion."

The apostle Paul knew that kind of passion. We groan for heaven, he said, not because we long to die but because we long to really live, to be with our Lord forever (2 Corinthians 5:6–8). But until then, "we live by faith, not by sight" (v. 7).

I recently heard about an elderly gentleman who was greeted in this way: "Nice to see you in the land of the living!" "Oh, I'm not in the land of the living," he replied. "I'm in the land of the dying. But I look forward to being in the land of the living soon when I'm in heaven." That man's heart is already there! Can that be said of you?

~~~

THE GAINS OF HEAVEN WILL MORE THAN COMPENSATE
FOR THE LOSSES OF EARTH.

We have sinned, even as our fathers did;
  we have done wrong and acted wickedly.
When our fathers were in Egypt,
  they gave no thought to your miracles;
they did not remember your many kindnesses,
  and they rebelled by the sea, the Red Sea.
Yet he saved them for his name's sake,
  to make his mighty power known.
He rebuked the Red Sea, and it dried up;
  he led them through the depths as through a desert.
He saved them from the hand of the foe;
  from the hand of the enemy he redeemed them.
The waters covered their adversaries;
  not one of them survived.
Then they believed his promises
  and sang his praise.
But they soon forgot what he had done
  and did not wait for his counsel.
In the desert they gave in to their craving;
  in the wasteland they put God to the test.
So he gave them what they asked for,
  but sent a wasting disease upon them.

PSALM 106:6-15

*W*ithout a doubt, this is a self-indulgent, demanding age. People want what they want, and they want it now. And when they get it, they only want more. That's true not only of undisciplined children but also of adults. "An undisciplined adult," wrote David Augsburger, "is just a child who has grown old."

A man named Bob admitted that he was always trying to get circumstances and people to be the way he wanted them to be. But he was frustrated because he was fighting a losing battle. One day he woke up to the fact that his life contained many good things just as it was. "When I think it through," he confessed, "I realize I'm spoiled. Maybe one of the definitions of a spoiled person is not knowing when to be satisfied."

This is not just a modern trend. Psalm 106 gives an honest confession of Israel's unfaithfulness. How quickly the people forgot God's great works and grumbled like spoiled children when they didn't get their way! Finally, when they tired of manna, God gave them the meat they demanded, but they soon regretted having asked for it (v. 15; Numbers 11:33).

Thank the Lord that He is able to deliver us from demanding, ungrateful attitudes. Oh, may we be fully satisfied with our gracious God.

CONTENTMENT IS WANTING WHAT WE HAVE.

Do you not know?
    Have you not heard?
The Lord is the everlasting God,
    the Creator of the ends of the earth.
He will not grow tired or weary,
    and his understanding no one can fathom.
He gives strength to the weary
    and increases the power of the weak.
Even youths grow tired and weary,
    and young men stumble and fall;
but those who hope in the Lord
    will renew their strength.
They will soar on wings like eagles;
    they will run and not grow weary,
    they will walk and not be faint.

ISAIAH 40:28-31

*T*oday's wife, mother, and homemaker is a professional juggler. She balances home, church, and community responsibilities and often runs a family taxi service.

My daughter Tina is a juggler who admits that she sometimes feels like resigning, but she's learned where to go with her struggle. Here's how it began.

One morning Tina woke up with the I-can't-juggle-it-all feeling and started to panic. Reaching for pen and paper, she began recording some spiritual "first aid," such as: "God is not stressed out. God is not frustrated. God is not exhausted. God is not confused. God is not panicking."

After listing what God is not, she began listing what He is: "God is relaxed. God's timing is perfect. God has continuous energy. God is in control. God knows everything." Then she wrote, "This God is living in me. He is working through me." By the time she wrote those words, Tina's panic feelings had flown. Before she had a chance to say, "God, I want to resign," she realized that He wanted to renew her strength.

Are you a juggler needing God's first aid for your soul? Guided by Isaiah 40:25–31, ponder the Lord's limitless attributes. Then let Him renew you.

～

BECAUSE GOD CARES ABOUT US,
WE CAN LEAVE OUR CARES WITH HIM.

*I sought the L*ORD*, and he answered me;*
  he delivered me from all my fears.
Those who look to him are radiant;
  their faces are never covered with shame.
*This poor man called, and the L*ORD *heard him;*
  he saved him out of all his troubles.
*The angel of the L*ORD *encamps around those who fear him,*
  and he delivers them.
*Taste and see that the L*ORD *is good;*
  blessed is the man who takes refuge in him.
*Fear the L*ORD*, you his saints,*
  for those who fear him lack nothing.
The lions may grow weak and hungry,
  *but those who seek the L*ORD *lack no good thing.*
Come, my children, listen to me;
  *I will teach you the fear of the L*ORD*.*
Whoever of you loves life
  and desires to see many good days,
keep your tongue from evil
  and your lips from speaking lies.
Turn from evil and do good;
  seek peace and pursue it.

PSALM 34:4–14

With appealing humor, Ron Hutchcraft, busy author, speaker, and counselor, tells about his battle with stress. One day Ron decided to "interview" the family gerbil.

"Tell me, Gerbie," Ron asked, "what do you have planned for today?"

"First, breakfast," he replied, "and then get started."

"Doing what?" Ron questioned.

"Why, the same thing I did yesterday and the day before that."

"What's that?" Ron asked again.

"The wheel."

And sure enough, Gerbie climbed on his little wheel and started running in circles. Hours later, he was still running.

The more Ron watched that gerbil, the more he saw himself. He had his own personal "wheels"—demands, deadlines, aggravations, ambitions. He felt as if he were running in circles, and he longed for peace. In his search he made this discovery in Psalm 34: Peace isn't automatic or passive; it must be pursued. Not only that, but peace is also a result of a right relationship with the Lord.

As never before, Ron enthroned the Lord as the Shepherd of his life. As he did, peace, instead of the stressful wheel, became normal. Which will be normal for you today?

~~~

FOR PEACE THAT LASTS, PUT GOD FIRST.

The end of all things is near. Therefore be clear minded and self-controlled so that you can pray. Above all, love each other deeply, because love covers over a multitude of sins. Offer hospitality to one another without grumbling. Each one should use whatever gift he has received to serve others, faithfully administering God's grace in its various forms. If anyone speaks, he should do it as one speaking the very words of God. If anyone serves, he should do it with the strength God provides, so that in all things God may be praised through Jesus Christ. To him be the glory and the power for ever and ever. Amen.

1 PETER 4:7-11

Our major highways are crawling with huge trucks, vans, and trailers. When we feel rushed, it's easy to see them as nothing more than a hindrance to those of us traveling in smaller vehicles. We forget that the drivers of these mighty carriers are stewards, serving you and me. Having collected all sorts of manufactured goods needed by people everywhere, they have only one aim: Deliver the goods. How impoverished we would be without their service!

The apostle Peter wrote that believers are called to be good stewards of God's vast resources. He called these resources "God's grace in its various forms" (1 Peter 4:10). The vehicle for receiving and delivering "God's goods" is a yielded life. And the uniqueness of that vehicle is determined by the particular ability God has given the individual. Once we dedicate that ability for His use and for Christ's glory, our aim should be to deliver the goods. If we fail to do so, others will not be blessed by our lives but will be starved instead.

Peter emphasized that the use of our gifts is a two-way ministry as we serve one another. As you journey life's road, don't look at other vehicles of God's grace as a hindrance. You could end up starving yourself and them.

~~

WE CAN NEVER DO TOO MUCH
FOR THE ONE WHO DID SO MUCH FOR US.

Although I am less than the least of all God's people, this grace was given me: to preach to the Gentiles the unsearchable riches of Christ, and to make plain to everyone the administration of this mystery, which for ages past was kept hidden in God, who created all things . . .

For this reason I kneel before the Father, from whom his whole family in heaven and on earth derives its name. I pray that out of his glorious riches he may strengthen you with power through his Spirit in your inner being, so that Christ may dwell in your hearts through faith. And I pray that you, being rooted and established in love, may have power, together with all the saints, to grasp how wide and long and high and deep is the love of Christ, and to know this love that surpasses knowledge—that you may be filled to the measure of all the fullness of God.

Now to him who is able to do immeasurably more than all we ask or imagine, according to his power that is at work within us, to him be glory in the church and in Christ Jesus throughout all generations, for ever and ever! Amen.

EPHESIANS 3:8-9, 14-21

During the Great Depression, a man named Mr. Yates owned a huge piece of land in Texas where he raised sheep. Financial problems had brought him to the brink of bankruptcy. Then an oil company, believing there might be oil on his land, asked for permission to drill.

With nothing to lose, Mr. Yates agreed. Soon, at a shallow depth, the workmen struck the largest oil deposit found at that time on the North American continent. Overnight, Mr. Yates became a billionaire. The amazing thing, though, is that the untapped riches were there all along. He just didn't know it!

Are you a spiritual "Mr. Yates" who is unaware of the riches you already own in Christ? When Paul wrote his letter to the Ephesians, he revealed hidden treasure by preaching "the unsearchable riches of Christ" (3:8). His goal was to make all Christians see how wealthy they actually are (v. 9).

Paul not only preached but also prayed that believers might recognize and use their spiritual wealth, that they would be strengthened within, established in love, powerful in prayer, and filled with God Himself.

Read Ephesians 3:14–21 again, and claim your unlimited spiritual resources today.

~~~

TO BE RICH IN GOD IS FAR BETTER
THAN TO BE RICH IN GOODS.

This is the word that came to Jeremiah from the LORD: "Go down to the potter's house, and there I will give you my message." So I went down to the potter's house, and I saw him working at the wheel. But the pot he was shaping from the clay was marred in his hands; so the potter formed it into another pot, shaping it as seemed best to him.

Then the word of the LORD came to me: "O house of Israel, can I not do with you as this potter does?" declares the LORD. "Like clay in the hand of the potter, so are you in my hand, O house of Israel. If at any time I announce that a nation or kingdom is to be uprooted, torn down and destroyed, and if that nation I warned repents of its evil, then I will relent and not inflict on it the disaster I had planned. And if at another time I announce that a nation or kingdom is to be built up and planted, and if it does evil in my sight and does not obey me, then I will reconsider the good I had intended to do for it.

"Now therefore say to the people of Judah and those living in Jerusalem, 'This is what the LORD says: Look! I am preparing a disaster for you and devising a plan against you. So turn from your evil ways, each one of you, and reform your ways and your actions.'"

JEREMIAH 18:1–11

When I first became a Christian, I thought my zeal would last a lifetime. But a few years later, as a missionary, wife, and mother, I had become a nerve-wracked, resentful, and doubting person. Having received Christ's good news for lost sinners at my conversion, I felt ashamed to long for more good news.

Then I read Jeremiah 18, and the Lord showed me that He still has good news for saved sinners like me. Our messed-up lives, like marred clay, can be refashioned if placed humbly in the Potter's hand.

Years later, I was attending a conference for Christian workers where Bible teacher Alan Redpath was speaking. His words reminded me of that new beginning. "I can't prove this by one particular verse," he said, "but I have a conviction supported by the entire Bible that God's great mercy to the unsaved is surpassed only by His mercy to the saved." At that moment, with years of God's mercy behind me, my spirit bore joyful witness to that truth. I realized that God's mercy is for Christians too!

Bring God your failures and receive His forgiveness now as freely as when you first believed. Your great Potter still loves you and longs to remake you.

~~~

GOD'S WORK IN US ISN'T OVER
WHEN WE RECEIVE CHRIST—
IT HAS JUST BEGUN.

[Titus] told us about your longing for me, your deep sorrow, your ardent concern for me, so that my joy was greater than ever.

Even if I caused you sorrow by my letter, I do not regret it. Though I did regret it—I see that my letter hurt you, but only for a little while—yet now I am happy, not because you were made sorry, but because your sorrow led you to repentance. For you became sorrowful as God intended and so were not harmed in any way by us. Godly sorrow brings repentance that leads to salvation and leaves no regret, but worldly sorrow brings death. See what this godly sorrow has produced in you: what earnestness, what eagerness to clear yourselves, what indignation, what alarm, what longing, what concern, what readiness to see justice done. At every point you have proved yourselves to be innocent in this matter. So even though I wrote to you, it was not on account of the one who did the wrong or of the injured party, but rather that before God you could see for yourselves how devoted to us you are. By all this we are encouraged.

In addition to our own encouragement, we were especially delighted to see how happy Titus was, because his spirit has been refreshed by all of you. I had boasted to him about you, and you have not embarrassed me. But just as everything we said to you was true, so our boasting about you to Titus has proved to be true as well. And his affection for you is all the greater when he remembers that you were all obedient, receiving him with fear and trembling. I am glad I can have complete confidence in you.

2 CORINTHIANS 7:7–16

*I*n Paul's second letter to the Christians in Corinth, he begins chapter 7 by calling them "dear friends" and finishes by rejoicing over his confidence in them.

How could he honestly say those things, considering that the rest of the chapter is about their sins he had sternly confronted in his first letter? (1 Corinthians 5). He could commend them because they had responded with godly sorrow. They had sincerely repented, and now their slate was completely clean!

Many of us as Christians find it difficult to accept God's forgiveness for our sin and to feel forgiven. We tell others about the love and forgiveness that Jesus offers, yet the hardest thing for us to do, it seems, is to receive that same love and forgiveness. After we've done something wrong, it's not unusual to feel sorry about it. But if we merely regret the consequences and don't genuinely repent and accept God's forgiveness, we have done nothing more than sorrow as the world does (2 Corinthians 7:10).

Don't say, "If only I could undo the past." You can't undo sin, but you can sincerely repent of it. Our merciful God is waiting right now to flood your troubled heart with the joy of His forgiveness.

～

GOD MAKES US MISERABLE THROUGH CONVICTION
TO MAKE US JOYFUL THROUGH CONFESSION.

Now I want you to know, brothers, that what has happened to me has really served to advance the gospel. As a result, it has become clear throughout the whole palace guard and to everyone else that I am in chains for Christ. Because of my chains, most of the brothers in the Lord have been encouraged to speak the word of God more courageously and fearlessly.

It is true that some preach Christ out of envy and rivalry, but others out of goodwill. The latter do so in love, knowing that I am put here for the defense of the gospel. The former preach Christ out of selfish ambition, not sincerely, supposing that they can stir up trouble for me while I am in chains. But what does it matter? The important thing is that in every way, whether from false motives or true, Christ is preached. And because of this I rejoice.

Yes, and I will continue to rejoice, for I know that through your prayers and the help given by the Spirit of Jesus Christ, what has happened to me will turn out for my deliverance. I eagerly expect and hope that I will in no way be ashamed, but will have sufficient courage so that now as always Christ will be exalted in my body, whether by life or by death. For me, to live is Christ and to die is gain.

PHILIPPIANS 1:12–21

vil men, not God, threw the apostle Paul into prison, hoping to put an end to his ministry. But their plan backfired, and the gospel spread (Philippians 1:12–13). Paul didn't know why God allowed his imprisonment, but he saw how God used it for good.

When All-Star baseball player Dave Dravecky lost his pitching arm to cancer, he struggled to find the reason for his loss by adding up the positive gains in his life. He eventually realized that he had been confusing the results of his loss with trying to understand God's unknowable purposes.

To illustrate the difference, Dave refers to his amputated arm. One result of his radical surgery was that medical researchers had cancerous tissue to study that could advance their knowledge of the disease. This is something good. "It wouldn't be such a good thing, though," Dave writes, "if the purpose for my surgery was to provide an arm so that the pathology department would have a specimen to study." That may be one result, but it doesn't explain God's higher purpose.

Instead of trying to discover God's hidden purpose for his cancer, Dave now focuses on a result that he has seen: "I used to depend on myself. Now I depend more on God."

WE CANNOT CONTROL THE WIND,
BUT WE CAN ADJUST OUR SAILS.

My heart is stirred by a noble theme
   as I recite my verses for the king;
   my tongue is the pen of a skillful writer.
You are the most excellent of men
   and your lips have been anointed with grace,
   since God has blessed you forever.
Gird your sword upon your side, O mighty one;
   clothe yourself with splendor and majesty.
In your majesty ride forth victoriously
   in behalf of truth, humility and righteousness;
   let your right hand display awesome deeds.
Let your sharp arrows pierce the hearts of the king's enemies;
   let the nations fall beneath your feet.
Your throne, O God, will last for ever and ever;
   a scepter of justice will be the scepter of your kingdom.
You love righteousness and hate wickedness;
   therefore God, your God, has set you above your companions
   by anointing you with the oil of joy.

PSALM 45:1–7

All of us as Christians who long to proclaim the riches of Christ and His good news know the limitations of having only one tongue. In one of his hymns, Charles Wesley wrote, "O for a thousand tongues to sing my great Redeemer's praise!"

The fact is, though, our one tongue has vastly greater potential than most of us will ever put to use. A tongue devoted to God can accomplish much.

For example, a man from Chicago was blind and had neither arms nor legs. But like the psalmist, his heart was overflowing with God's love, and his tongue was fully dedicated for His use. This man learned to read the Braille Bible using his tongue! As a result of this painstaking accomplishment, he was able to use his tongue in a different way—to teach the Word of God and to share his radiant testimony.

Joni Eareckson Tada, another believer with physical disabilities, has spoken to millions about Christ. She often affirms, "With God, less is more."

Are you sometimes discouraged, thinking that you have little to offer to God? If you have Christ's love in your heart and a willing tongue in your mouth, offer them boldly to God today and begin to bring praise and honor to the Lord. One tongue is enough.

~~~

LITTLE IS MUCH WHEN GOD IS IN IT.

He was in the world, and the world was made through Him, and the world did not know Him.

He came to His own, and His own did not receive Him.

But as many as received Him, to them He gave the right to become children of God, to those who believe in His name: who were born, not of blood, nor of the will of the flesh, nor of the will of man, but of God.

And the Word became flesh and dwelt among us, and we beheld His glory, the glory as of the only begotten of the Father, full of grace and truth.

John bore witness of Him and cried out, saying, "This was He of whom I said, 'He who comes before me is preferred before me, for He was before me.'"

And of His fullness we have all received, and grace for grace.

For the law was given through Moses, but grace and truth came through Jesus Christ.

No one has seen God at any time. The only begotten Son, who is in the bosom of the Father, He has declared Him.

JOHN 1:10–18, NKJV

I once heard someone describe his troublesome life like this: "Each day is just yesterday warmed up!" Yes, life sometimes dishes up a diet of old problems disguised as new ones. It's like the frugal housewife who feeds her family for a week on leftovers from Sunday dinner, serving the same old food in different disguises.

It was into such a tiresome, troublesome world that Jesus came. The apostle John said that Jesus is full of grace and truth, and He supplies us with "grace for grace" (1:14, 16).

Years ago, Amy Carmichael shared some helpful insights about the phrase "grace for grace." Drawing from the writings of Bishop Moule (1841–1920), she wrote that the Greek word translated "for" literally means "instead of." He illustrated the meaning by describing a river. "Stand on its banks," he wrote, "and contemplate the flow of waters. A minute passes, and another. Is it the same stream still? Yes. But is it the same water? No." The old water, he explained, had been displaced by new—"water instead of water."

The same is true of grace. Your life today may carry yesterday's problems, but remember, God's grace is new each morning, exactly what you need to meet each new challenge. It is an inexhaustible and ever-fresh supply.

GOD GIVES SPECIAL GRACE FOR EACH TRIAL WE FACE.

I love you, O Lord, my strength.

The Lord is my rock, my fortress and my deliverer;
    my God is my rock, in whom I take refuge.
    He is my shield and the horn of my salvation, my stronghold.
I call to the Lord, who is worthy of praise,
    and I am saved from my enemies.
The cords of death entangled me;
    the torrents of destruction overwhelmed me.
The cords of the grave coiled around me;
    the snares of death confronted me.
In my distress I called to the Lord;
    I cried to my God for help.
From his temple he heard my voice;
    my cry came before him, into his ears . . .

He reached down from on high and took hold of me;
    he drew me out of deep waters.
He rescued me from my powerful enemy,
    from my foes, who were too strong for me.
They confronted me in the day of my disaster,
    but the Lord was my support.
He brought me out into a spacious place;
    he rescued me because he delighted in me.

PSALM 18:1-6, 16-19

*W*hen someone loves another, there is a compelling desire to express it. Hence those timeless words: "How do I love thee? Let me count the ways!"

I wonder, when do we feel compelled to express sincere, overflowing love to our Lord? It takes different things for different people, but God's personal dealings in our lives are designed to generate a renewed love for Him.

One instance of God's work in my life stands out in my memory. Due to mounting pressures in my life, my energies were slowly ebbing away and love for God was far from my mind. Although I wasn't thinking of Psalm 18 at the time, I did what David did in verse 6: "I called to the LORD; I cried to my God for help." Applied to my stormy situation, verse 16 could be worded like this: "The Lord sent me strength from above and kept me from sinking beneath waves of human weakness." Oh, how I loved Him then, not only because He had given me strength but because God was my strength.

Think back to the Lord's special work in your life. Or call on Him for today's needs. Then compose your own psalm of love: "I love You, O LORD, my . . ."

~~~

TO RENEW YOUR LOVE FOR CHRIST,
REVIEW CHRIST'S LOVE FOR YOU.

That same day the Sadducees, who say there is no resurrection, came to him with a question. "Teacher," they said, "Moses told us that if a man dies without having children, his brother must marry the widow and have children for him. Now there were seven brothers among us. The first one married and died, and since he had no children, he left his wife to his brother. The same thing happened to the second and third brother, right on down to the seventh. Finally, the woman died. Now then, at the resurrection, whose wife will she be of the seven, since all of them were married to her?"

Jesus replied, "You are in error because you do not know the Scriptures or the power of God. At the resurrection people will neither marry nor be given in marriage; they will be like the angels in heaven. But about the resurrection of the dead—have you not read what God said to you, 'I am the God of Abraham, the God of Isaac, and the God of Jacob'? He is not the God of the dead but of the living."

When the crowds heard this, they were astonished at his teaching.

MATTHEW 22:23-33

After the death of her beloved husband, a certain Christian woman felt saddened by these words of Jesus: "At the resurrection people will neither marry nor be given in marriage" (Matthew 22:30). Intensely missing her husband and the life they had enjoyed together, she thought of heaven without marriage as drab compared with the satisfying life she and her husband cherished on earth.

During the early days of my own widowhood, I fully accepted the reality of heaven without marriage. Yet I felt I was overlooking something vital. And I was! While meditating one day on God's promises about heaven, my earthbound brain woke up to the realization that Jesus didn't say heaven would be without marriage, only without earthly marriage. In Revelation 19:6–9, we're told that everyone heading for heaven is heading for a celestial wedding, banquet and all! It's the long-planned marriage of God's Lamb to His long-prepared bride, God's redeemed people.

As we continue to get ready for it, let's remember this: Although the marriage of the Lamb is wonderfully foreshadowed by Christian marriage on earth (Ephesians 5:23– 27), it is an event all redeemed people can look forward to. It's our wedding!

~

AMEN. COME. LORD JESUS.—REVELATION 22:20

Sorrow is better than laughter,
*   because a sad face is good for the heart.*
The heart of the wise is in the house of mourning,
but the heart of fools is in the house of pleasure.
It is better to heed a wise man's rebuke
*   than to listen to the song of fools.*
Like the crackling of thorns under the pot,
*   so is the laughter of fools.*
*   This too is meaningless. . .*
When times are good, be happy;
*   but when times are bad, consider:*
God has made the one
*   as well as the other.*
Therefore, a man cannot discover
*   anything about his future.*

ECCLESIASTES 7:3-6; 14

We've all had our share of both laughter and sorrow. Although we naturally enjoy laughter more than tears, we would have to say that most of the wisdom we've gained along the way we owe to the sad times. Yet many Christians are obsessed with the pursuit of personal happiness. The writer of Ecclesiastes rated such a pursuit as foolish (7:3–4).

Several years ago in an interview during his battle with cancer, theologian Francis Schaeffer said, "The only way to be foolishly happy in this world is to be young enough, well enough, and have money enough—and not give a care about other people. But as soon as you don't have any of the first three, or if you have compassion for the weeping world around you, then it is impossible to have the foolish kind of happiness that I believe some Christians present as Christianity."

What is our greatest need in life? Is it to be happy? We may long for a change in our circumstances, and sometimes that's what we get. But a changed life is our deepest need. Changed circumstances may make us happier, but a changed life will make us better, for it will make us like Christ.

What is your main pursuit in life?

～～～

HAPPINESS IS NOT THE GOAL OF LIFE—GODLINESS IS.

For God so loved the world that he gave his one and only Son, that whoever believes in him shall not perish but have eternal life. For God did not send his Son into the world to condemn the world, but to save the world through him. Whoever believes in him is not condemned, but whoever does not believe stands condemned already because he has not believed in the name of God's one and only Son. This is the verdict: Light has come into the world, but men loved darkness instead of light because their deeds were evil. Everyone who does evil hates the light, and will not come into the light for fear that his deeds will be exposed. But whoever lives by the truth comes into the light, so that it may be seen plainly that what he has done has been done through God.

JOHN 3:16–21

*I*n John 3:16 we read, "For God so loved the world." But what about His love for individuals? The rest of the verse reveals the central purpose behind God's sacrifice of His Son: "That whoever believes in him shall not perish but have eternal life." Therefore, without exception, every person may interpret John 3:16 like this: "For God so loved me!"

A. B. Simpson, a great missionary of the past, often hugged a globe to his chest and wept over the world's lostness. Yet his global vision was marked by compassion for individuals. You and I also must feel the responsibility to take the gospel to our world—by sharing the good news with one person at a time.

Unfortunately, we often think of the Great Commission in terms of "foreign missions" only. "World missions" is perhaps a better term, for that includes our nearest neighbors, who are part of the world to which God has called us. And we are already there!

Like A. B. Simpson, embrace your smaller world through earnest prayer as you consider lost individuals in your family, neighborhood, and workplace. Then, as you seek to live and give the good news, expect God to open doors of opportunity.

~

THE LIGHT THAT SHINES FARTHEST,
SHINES BRIGHTEST AT HOME.

A certain ruler asked him, "Good teacher, what must I do to inherit eternal life?"

"Why do you call me good?" Jesus answered. "No one is good—except God alone. You know the commandments: 'Do not commit adultery, do not murder, do not steal, do not give false testimony, honor your father and mother.'"

"All these I have kept since I was a boy," he said.

When Jesus heard this, he said to him, "You still lack one thing. Sell everything you have and give to the poor, and you will have treasure in heaven. Then come, follow me."

When he heard this, he became very sad, because he was a man of great wealth. Jesus looked at him and said, "How hard it is for the rich to enter the kingdom of God! Indeed, it is easier for a camel to go through the eye of a needle than for a rich man to enter the kingdom of God."

Those who heard this asked, "Who then can be saved?"

Jesus replied, "What is impossible with men is possible with God."

LUKE 18:18–27

Countless times I've heard myself say, "I'm going to bake a cake." Then one day I realized that I've never baked a cake in my life—only my oven can do that. I simply mix the right ingredients and allow the oven to do its part. Through that division of labor, I have the joy of seeing others taste and enjoy delicious cake.

God used my mixing-bowl musings to clarify a dilemma I once had after starting a neighborhood Bible study. It was one thing to bring my neighbors together to study the Bible, but seeing them believe and follow Christ was another. I felt powerless. Suddenly I saw the obvious. Like baking cakes, making Christians was impossible for me, but not for God. I had blended the right ingredients—an open home, friendship, love. Now I had to trust the Holy Spirit, through His Word, to do His work. When I cooperated with that division of labor, I had the joy of seeing others taste of God's goodness.

In Luke 18:18–27, Jesus so vividly described some hindrances to saving faith that His listeners began to wonder if anyone could be saved. Do you feel that way about someone? Be encouraged by the Lord's strong reminder that there are some things that only God can do. Saving people is one of them.

WE SOW THE SEED, BUT GOD BRINGS THE HARVEST.

I lift up my eyes to the hills—
*   where does my help come from?*
My help comes from the LORD,
*   the Maker of heaven and earth.*
He will not let your foot slip—
*   he who watches over you will not slumber;*
indeed, he who watches over Israel
*   will neither slumber nor sleep.*
The LORD watches over you—
*   the LORD is your shade at your right hand;*
the sun will not harm you by day,
*   nor the moon by night.*
The LORD will keep you from all harm—
*   he will watch over your life;*
the LORD will watch over your coming and going
*   both now and forevermore.*

PSALM 121

My husband and I were committed to having a "people ministry." We longed to bring Christ's good news to needy people and to be good news through our day-to-day involvement with them. The snag was that I was "working the night shift" as well by carrying people's burdens to bed with me. My restless nights often immobilized me during the day.

One night as I was getting ready for bed, I was thinking about my burdens and what to do with them. As I laid aside each piece of clothing, I decided to lay aside each concern, one by one. Then, as I put on my comfortable robe, I felt released from people's burdens and ready to rest. At first I felt guilty and uncaring. Then the Holy Spirit reminded me that God neither slumbers nor sleeps. If God wanted me to be involved during the night, He would let me know. Otherwise, while I slept and refreshed myself, I knew that He would sit up all night and keep watch over my every concern.

If you're a believer, you too have a "people ministry." But remember, you don't need to work the night shift. Instead, practice laying aside your concerns daily, like pieces of apparel. Then wrap yourself in the reassuring robe of God's keeping power and rest awhile.

~~~

FOR A GOOD NIGHT'S REST, REST IN THE LORD.

*Then the L*ORD *called Samuel.*

Samuel answered, "Here I am." And he ran to Eli and said, "Here I am; you called me."

But Eli said, "I did not call; go back and lie down." So he went and lay down.

*Again the L*ORD *called, "Samuel!" And Samuel got up and went to Eli and said, "Here I am; you called me."*

"My son," Eli said, "I did not call; go back and lie down."

*Now Samuel did not yet know the L*ORD*: The word of the L*ORD *had not yet been revealed to him.*

*The L*ORD *called Samuel a third time, and Samuel got up and went to Eli and said, "Here I am; you called me."*

*Then Eli realized that the L*ORD *was calling the boy. So Eli told Samuel, "Go and lie down, and if he calls you, say, 'Speak, L*ORD*, for your servant is listening.' " So Samuel went and lay down in his place.*

*The L*ORD *came and stood there, calling as at the other times, "Samuel! Samuel!"*

Then Samuel said, "Speak, for your servant is listening."

1 SAMUEL 3:4-10

*J*oshua, a precocious two-year-old, watched his mother baking cookies. "Please, may I have one?" he asked hopefully. "Not before supper," his mother replied. Joshua ran tearfully to his room, then reappeared with this message: "Jesus just told me it's okay to have a cookie now." "Jesus didn't tell me!" his mother retorted, to which Joshua replied, "You must not have been listening!"

Joshua's motivation was wrong, but he was absolutely right about two things: God longs to speak to us, and we need to listen.

In 1 Samuel 3, another young boy learned those same ageless principles. When Samuel followed Eli's counsel and prayed, "Speak, LORD, for your servant is listening," he was open to receiving God's powerful message (v. 10). Like Samuel, we long to hear God speaking to us but often fail to discern His voice.

God spoke audibly to Samuel. Today He speaks to us by His Spirit through the Scriptures, other people, and our circumstances. But as a result of neglect and nonstop activity, some of us have become "hard of hearing." We need a "spiritual hearing aid." There is one in Samuel's prayer: "Speak, for your servant is listening" (v. 10). This humble attitude is a real help for the spiritually hard of hearing.

~~~

GOD SPEAKS THROUGH HIS WORD.
TAKE TIME TO LISTEN.

At that time the disciples came to Jesus and asked, "Who is the greatest in the kingdom of heaven?"

He called a little child and had him stand among them. And he said: "I tell you the truth, unless you change and become like little children, you will never enter the kingdom of heaven. Therefore, whoever humbles himself like this child is the greatest in the kingdom of heaven.

"And whoever welcomes a little child like this in my name welcomes me. But if anyone causes one of these little ones who believe in me to sin, it would be better for him to have a large millstone hung around his neck and to be drowned in the depths of the sea."

MATTHEW 18:1-6

*I*n the mid-1970s, my husband Bill and I befriended a drug addict named Derek on the London subway. Days later we invited him to come and live with our family. He soon received Christ and His forgiveness.

Until then, the world had been shouting to Derek, "Why don't you grow up?" That day Jesus tenderly said to him, "Unless you change and become like little children, you will never enter the kingdom of heaven" (Matthew 18:3). Derek became a child of God! We expected this young man to learn a lot through us about God, but little did we expect to learn about God through him.

For example, one afternoon we discussed the possibility of someday opening a Christian rehabilitation center for addicts. None of us knew when, where, how, or if it would ever happen. I said, "Well, we know God won't let us down." Derek, however, added, "God won't let Himself down." His words echoed Psalm 23:3, "He guides me in paths of righteousness for His name's sake."

Twenty eventful years ago He brought that rehabilitation center into being "for His name's sake," and I've been learning and relearning childlike humility ever since. How about you?

~~~

IF YOU'RE FILLED WITH PRIDE,
YOU WON'T HAVE ROOM FOR WISDOM.

Do you not know?
Have you not heard?
The LORD is the everlasting God,
the Creator of the ends of the earth.
He will not grow tired or weary,
and his understanding no one can fathom.
He gives strength to the weary
and increases the power of the weak.
Even youths grow tired and weary,
and young men stumble and fall;
but those who hope in the LORD
will renew their strength.
They will soar on wings like eagles;
they will run and not grow weary,
they will walk and not be faint.

ISAIAH 40:28-31

Someone confided in me that she was feeling guilty. She said, "Even though I'm a Christian, I still get so tired!" As I reviewed the Scriptures, I found that God's people sometimes suffered fatigue and even exhaustion. Today's church seems unwilling to acknowledge this, however. In the name of victorious Christian living, some view all weariness as a failure to trust and obey God.

But according to Isaiah, our Creator anticipates weariness in His finite creatures. He promises to renew our strength if we wait on Him (40:30–31). He also understands that our need for strength, like our need for food, isn't a once-for-all provision.

Our choice is not whether we will experience weariness but what we will be weary about. In my own life, I suffered exhaustion during a long period of time because of worry, fear, and bitterness. Thanks to the Lord, these negative feelings no longer dominate me. But I still get very tired because of my involvement in worthy causes and my desire to live faithfully as a servant of Christ.

Give yourself a "tiredness test." If you are tired for the wrong reasons, humbly seek God's loving correction. If you are tired for the right reasons, seek God's renewing strength. You don't need to feel guilty about feeling weary.

~

GOD GIVES STRENGTH
IN PROPORTION TO THE STRAIN.

The time is coming, declares the Lord,
  when I will make a new covenant
with the house of Israel
  and with the house of Judah.
It will not be like the covenant
  I made with their forefathers
when I took them by the hand
  to lead them out of Egypt,
because they did not remain faithful to my covenant,
  and I turned away from them,

                    declares the Lord.
This is the covenant I will make with the house of Israel
  after that time, declares the Lord.
I will put my laws in their minds
  and write them on their hearts.
I will be their God,
  and they will be my people.
No longer will a man teach his neighbor,
  or a man his brother, saying, 'Know the Lord,'
because they will all know me,
  from the least of them to the greatest.
For I will forgive their wickedness
  and will remember their sins no more.

HEBREWS 8:8–12

God longs to forgive sinners! But in the minds of many people, this thought seems too good to be true. Countless sermons have been preached to convince guilt-ridden individuals that it is true. Many of these sermons emphasize the idea that God not only forgives the sinner, but He also forgets the sin. I've often said it myself, never doubting its soundness.

Then one Sunday I heard a sermon that revolutionized my thinking. The speaker caught my attention when he said, "The idea that God forgets my sins isn't very reassuring to me. After all, what if He suddenly remembered? In any case, only imperfection can forget, and God is perfect."

As I was questioning the biblical basis for such statements, the pastor read Hebrews 8:12, "For I will forgive their wickedness and will remember their sins no more." Then he said, "God doesn't say He'll forget our sins—He says He'll remember them no more! His promise not to remember them ever again is stronger than saying He'll forget them. Now that reassures me!"

Do you feel that you are too bad to be forgiven? Remember, God promises to forgive and never bring up your sin against you. Confess it to Him now.

~~

TO ENJOY THE FUTURE,
ACCEPT GOD'S FORGIVENESS FOR THE PAST.

As apostles of Christ we could have been a burden to you, but we were gentle among you, like a mother caring for her little children. We loved you so much that we were delighted to share with you not only the gospel of God but our lives as well, because you had become so dear to us. Surely you remember, brothers, our toil and hardship; we worked night and day in order not to be a burden to anyone while we preached the gospel of God to you.

You are witnesses, and so is God, of how holy, righteous and blameless we were among you who believed. For you know that we dealt with each of you as a father deals with his own children, encouraging, comforting and urging you to live lives worthy of God, who calls you into his kingdom and glory.

And we also thank God continually because, when you received the word of God, which you heard from us, you accepted it not as the word of men, but as it actually is, the word of God, which is at work in you who believe.

1 THESSALONIANS 2:6–13

*S*ome parents raise their children with harsh authority, but wise parents exercise their authority with lots of TLC — tender loving care!

Paul and his co-workers, Silvanus and Timothy, were spiritual parents to God's family in the Thessalonian church. Paul said, "We were gentle among you, like a mother caring for her little children" (1 Thessalonians 2:7). And he spoke of exhorting, comforting, and admonishing them "as a father deals with his own children" (v. 11). Like all Christian mothers and fathers, Paul desired that his spiritual children would grow up to reflect God's glory.

Bible commentator Albert Barnes wrote, "Those who minister the gospel should be gentle, tender, and affectionate . . . What is wrong we should indeed oppose — but it should be in the kindest manner toward those who do wrong."

In other words, we are to hate the sin but love the sinner. That's not easy, especially among those we know best. For author C. S. Lewis, it seemed impossible until he remembered: "There was a man to whom I had been doing this all my life — namely myself!"

Let's apply that principle toward others today and rediscover the power of truth joined with tenderness.

~~

WHEN TRUTH IS MIXED WITH TENDERNESS,
IT'S EASIER TO TAKE.

Then the angel who talked with me returned and wakened me, as a man is wakened from his sleep. He asked me, "What do you see?"

I answered, "I see a solid gold lampstand with a bowl at the top and seven lights on it, with seven channels to the lights. Also there are two olive trees by it, one on the right of the bowl and the other on its left."

I asked the angel who talked with me, "What are these, my lord?"

He answered, "Do you not know what these are?"

"No, my lord," I replied.

So he said to me, "This is the word of the Lord to Zerubbabel: 'Not by might nor by power, but by my Spirit,' says the Lord Almighty.

"What are you, O mighty mountain? Before Zerubbabel you will become level ground. Then he will bring out the capstone to shouts of 'God bless it! God bless it!' "

Then the word of the Lord came to me: "The hands of Zerubbabel have laid the foundation of this temple; his hands will also complete it. Then you will know that the Lord Almighty has sent me to you.

"Who despises the day of small things? Men will rejoice when they see the plumb line in the hand of Zerubbabel.

"(These seven are the eyes of the Lord, which range throughout the earth.)"

ZECHARIAH 4:1–10

*I*n his book *No Little People*, theologian Francis Schaeffer wrote: "In God's sight there are no little people and no little places . . . Those who think of themselves as little people in little places, if committed to Christ and living under His lordship in the whole of life, may, by God's grace, change the flow of our generation."

The attitude that our work is insignificant is common to homemakers, laborers, students, and countless others who serve quietly. When our efforts go unnoticed, we may feel like little people, filling little places, performing little deeds.

In Zechariah 4:9 we read that Zerubbabel had built the temple's foundation. Building foundations requires hard work and forward-looking faith. Yet some considered Zerubbabel's work insignificant, so God challenged them: "Who despises the day of small things?" (Zechariah 4:10). God wanted them to go on laying brick upon brick, following Zerubbabel's example. They were to fulfill the task through the enablement of God's Spirit, not in their own power (v. 6).

Are you doing "small things"? Be encouraged! God's eyes scan "throughout the earth" (v. 10). He notices the little things done for Him, and He will use them mightily.

THE DEWDROP DOES GOD'S WORK
AS MUCH AS THE THUNDERSTORM.

Why are you downcast, O my soul?
    Why so disturbed within me?
Put your hope in God,
    for I will yet praise him,
    my Savior and my God.
My soul is downcast within me;
    therefore I will remember you
from the land of the Jordan,
    the heights of Hermon—from Mount Mizar.
Deep calls to deep
    in the roar of your waterfalls;
all your waves and breakers
    have swept over me.
By day the LORD directs his love,
    at night his song is with me—
    a prayer to the God of my life.

PSALM 42:5–8

Talking to oneself is something many people ridicule in others and vow they'll never do themselves. They assume it's a sign of losing touch with reality. In light of what we read today in Psalm 42, though, let's think about it.

Before the psalmist talked to God about his depressed soul, he talked to his depressed soul about God. He said, "Why are you downcast, O my soul? Why so disturbed within me? Put your hope in God, for I will yet praise Him, my Savior and my God" (v. 5). David was talking to himself, but he certainly was not losing his mind. His words sound like someone in touch with reality!

Once I urged a new Christian to testify to others about the change that Jesus had made in his life. I knew that his own faith would be encouraged as he talked to others. He agreed with my suggestion, but he surprised me by saying, "I even testify to myself!"

When you're depressed, remember to take advantage of the spiritual antidepressants in Psalm 42. Question your soul, testify about God's goodness, admonish yourself to hope in the Lord. Minister to yourself, as David did, by personally applying the very encouragement you've given to others.

TO CHANGE YOUR OUTLOOK,
REMEMBER WHO'S LOOKING OUT FOR YOU.

As for you, you were dead in your transgressions and sins, in which you used to live when you followed the ways of this world and of the ruler of the kingdom of the air, the spirit who is now at work in those who are disobedient. All of us also lived among them at one time, gratifying the cravings of our sinful nature and following its desires and thoughts. Like the rest, we were by nature objects of wrath. But because of his great love for us, God, who is rich in mercy, made us alive with Christ even when we were dead in transgressions—it is by grace you have been saved. And God raised us up with Christ and seated us with him in the heavenly realms in Christ Jesus, in order that in the coming ages he might show the incomparable riches of his grace, expressed in his kindness to us in Christ Jesus. For it is by grace you have been saved, through faith—and this not from yourselves, it is the gift of God—not by works, so that no one can boast. For we are God's workmanship, created in Christ Jesus to do good works, which God prepared in advance for us to do.

EPHESIANS 2:1–10

Many people assume that we qualify for heaven by doing good deeds. This fallacy is illustrated by a comment made after the death of a man who had been held in high esteem. A friend said, "If anyone goes to heaven, he'll certainly be there, for he was such a good man!"

According to the apostle Paul, however, salvation is based on God's gift of grace and not on good works that anyone can boast about (Ephesians 2:8–9). So where, then, do works belong? In the next verse, Paul described believers as "created in Christ Jesus to do good works [not by good works], which God prepared in advance for us to do" (v. 10).

If we're not straight on this matter, we'll make the mistake of trying to earn our way into heaven, which the Bible says no one can do (Romans 3:23–28). How does grace deal with this problem? An elderly man on his deathbed said it well: "I have just taken all my good works and all my bad works and thrown them right overboard, and I am going to heaven on the basis of free grace."

The only safe and sure foundation for both life and death is God's free gift of grace. That's not cheap grace, however, for remember that Jesus died to pay the penalty for our sin. We are saved for good works.

~~~

WE ARE NOT SAVED BY GOOD WORKS
BUT FOR GOOD WORKS.

When I kept silent,
   my bones wasted away
   through my groaning all day long.
For day and night
   your hand was heavy upon me;
my strength was sapped
   as in the heat of summer. Selah
Then I acknowledged my sin to you
   and did not cover up my iniquity.
I said, "I will confess
   my transgressions to the LORD"—
and you forgave
   the guilt of my sin. Selah. . . .
I will instruct you and teach you in the way you should go;
   I will counsel you and watch over you.
Do not be like the horse or the mule,
   which have no understanding
but must be controlled by bit and bridle
   or they will not come to you.
Many are the woes of the wicked,
   but the LORD's unfailing love
   surrounds the man who trusts in him.

PSALM 32:3-5, 8-10

Some people's hair has a will of its own. It knows where it wants to go and stubbornly resists all attempts to make it go elsewhere. Others have very manageable hair. It willingly does whatever the stylist decides it should do. It knows who's boss and gladly receives all the help it can get. With that help, results can be astounding.

People can be self-willed too. Psalm 32 says that we can sometimes be like a horse or a mule that lacks understanding (v. 9). God knows we need all the help we can get, so He longs for us to give Him control of our lives. He wants to instruct us in the way we should go and guide us with His watchful eye (v. 8).

Those who yield to God's purposes are not spineless. Having made God's will their own, theirs is the strongest will possible. By exchanging their own agenda for God's, their lives produce some amazing, God-glorifying results.

Whose agenda are you following—yours or God's? David, the composer of today's psalm, knew the futility of living for himself (vv. 3–5). As you submit to the Lord's direction, you'll prove in your own experience what David found to be true in his: God's mercy surrounds the person who surrenders to Him (v. 10).

~~~

TO MAKE SOMETHING OF YOUR LIFE,
GIVE YOUR LIFE TO GOD.

To keep me from becoming conceited because of these surpassingly great revelations, there was given me a thorn in my flesh, a messenger of Satan, to torment me. Three times I pleaded with the Lord to take it away from me. But he said to me, "My grace is sufficient for you, for my power is made perfect in weakness." Therefore I will boast all the more gladly about my weaknesses, so that Christ's power may rest on me. That is why, for Christ's sake, I delight in weaknesses, in insults, in hardships, in persecutions, in difficulties. For when I am weak, then I am strong.

2 CORINTHIANS 12:1–10

*F*anny Crosby, composer of thousands of songs, was truly "more than a conqueror." When she was only six weeks old, faulty treatment of an eye infection resulted in lifelong blindness. By age eight, having fought and won over discouragement, she wrote this poem:

> Oh what a happy soul I am,
> Although I cannot see;
> I am resolved that in this world
> Contented I will be.

Instead of weeping and sighing, Fanny Crosby dedicated her blindness to God. Out of her rich Christian experience she composed numerous gospel hymns. In her testimonial song "Blessed Assurance," she seemed to forget that she was blind. Phrases like "Visions of rapture now burst on my sight" or "Watching and waiting, looking above" expressed what she called "a foretaste of glory divine."

While many of us seek Christ for what we can get, Fanny Crosby sought Christ for what she could become through Him—more than a conqueror (Romans 8:37). Even through times of extreme distress, God's grace is sufficient (2 Corinthians 12:9), and He is lovingly working to make us more like His Son.

We all need to ask ourselves: Is our Christian life about getting or becoming?

~~

SEEK CHRIST NOT FOR WHAT YOU CAN GET
BUT FOR WHAT YOU CAN BECOME.

Then Jesus said to his disciples: "Therefore I tell you, do not worry about your life, what you will eat; or about your body, what you will wear. Life is more than food, and the body more than clothes. Consider the ravens: They do not sow or reap, they have no storeroom or barn; yet God feeds them. And how much more valuable you are than birds! Who of you by worrying can add a single hour to his life? Since you cannot do this very little thing, why do you worry about the rest?

"Consider how the lilies grow. They do not labor or spin. Yet I tell you, not even Solomon in all his splendor was dressed like one of these. If that is how God clothes the grass of the field, which is here today, and tomorrow is thrown into the fire, how much more will he clothe you, O you of little faith! And do not set your heart on what you will eat or drink; do not worry about it. For the pagan world runs after all such things, and your Father knows that you need them. But seek his kingdom, and these things will be given to you as well.

"Do not be afraid, little flock, for your Father has been pleased to give you the kingdom."

LUKE 12:22–32

*T*ime and time again, the Lord has tenderly spoken these reassuring words to His people: "Do not be afraid." Yet how prone we are to live our days, like frightened lambs, in fear and anxiety.

Why are we fearful? Could it be that we see God as a reluctant giver?

Jesus tenderly corrected this distortion when He said, "Do not be afraid, little flock, for your Father has been pleased to give you the kingdom" (Luke 12:32). When Jesus said, "Do not be afraid," He implied that fear is needless because we can trust our Father's care.

Not too long ago, I was stewing about several personal concerns while driving my car. Suddenly the words "Do not be afraid!" broke into my troubled mind. As my car ate up the miles, God's loving rebuke ate up my doubts, and I prayed, "Lord, when You said, 'Do not be afraid,' You really meant it! You want me to take You seriously, and that means trusting the Father's eagerness to look after me and my needs."

Jesus said that our heavenly Father knows what we need, and if we seek His kingdom first His provisions will be ours (vv. 30–31). We can trust Him. He meant what He said.

~~~

THE PERFECT CURE FOR FEAR IS TRUST IN GOD.

Although I am less than the least of all God's people, this grace was given me: to preach to the Gentiles the unsearchable riches of Christ, and to make plain to everyone the administration of this mystery, which for ages past was kept hidden in God, who created all things . . .

I pray that out of his glorious riches he may strengthen you with power through his Spirit in your inner being, so that Christ may dwell in your hearts through faith. And I pray that you, being rooted and established in love, may have power, together with all the saints, to grasp how wide and long and high and deep is the love of Christ, and to know this love that surpasses knowledge—that you may be filled to the measure of all the fullness of God.

Now to him who is able to do immeasurably more than all we ask or imagine, according to his power that is at work within us, to him be glory in the church and in Christ Jesus throughout all generations, for ever and ever! Amen.

EPHESIANS 3:8, 16–21

What makes the gospel such good news? Paul summarized it in Ephesians 3:8 as "the unsearchable riches of Christ." Those who receive the living Christ into their lives are free to enjoy His spiritual riches. But are we using all that He has given to us?

Author Bob George has observed that it's possible for a Christian to live as a "practical atheist." That's a person who, despite right doctrine, "approaches life as if he were the only resource available." Such an approach is as unnecessary and impractical as buying a powerful car and then pushing it.

The apostle Paul's passion for the Ephesian believers was that they might realize that Christ's resources could meet all their needs. He prayed for them and asked God the Father to give them spiritual strength, close fellowship with Christ, and better understanding of His love for them, resulting in greater Christlikeness (Ephesians 3:16–19). He prayed because he believed our God is able to do "immeasurably more than all we ask or imagine" (v. 20).

Are you enjoying Christ's treasures? Or are you pushing on in your own strength? Paul's prayer gives us reason to be thankful. God has everything we need.

~~~

GOD WANTS TO BE EVERYTHING TO EVERY ONE OF US
AT EVERY MOMENT.

But now a righteousness from God, apart from law, has been made known, to which the Law and the Prophets testify. This righteousness from God comes through faith in Jesus Christ to all who believe. There is no difference, for all have sinned and fall short of the glory of God, and are justified freely by his grace through the redemption that came by Christ Jesus. God presented him as a sacrifice of atonement, through faith in his blood. He did this to demonstrate his justice, because in his forbearance he had left the sins committed beforehand unpunished—he did it to demonstrate his justice at the present time, so as to be just and the one who justifies those who have faith in Jesus.

Where, then, is boasting? It is excluded. On what principle? On that of observing the law? No, but on that of faith. For we maintain that a man is justified by faith apart from observing the law.

ROMANS 3:21–28

*P*raise God that He has not withdrawn His offer of forgiveness for sin! This good news, however, is for sinners only. Many people, though, don't see themselves as sinners in need of salvation. They make excuses like these:

- My good deeds outweigh my bad.
- I'm not as bad as some people.
- Usually I'm a good person.

Their shortcomings, they feel, don't jeopardize their standing before Almighty God.

Imagine a citizen being brought to trial for several charges of shoplifting. It would be useless for that person to appeal to the judge by saying: "Don't forget, my good deeds outweigh my bad." "I'm not as bad as many others." "Most of the time I'm a law-abiding citizen." The offender must be judged according to the offense, not according to previous good deeds. If justice is to be done, someone must pay, and that someone should be the offender—unless another is allowed to bear the penalty instead. That's exactly what Christ in love did for sinners, which we all are, "for all have sinned and fall short of the glory of God" (Romans 3:23).

Has false reasoning kept you from the One who died and rose again for you? If so, He's waiting for you to admit your need and put your trust in Him.

~

IF YOU SAY, "I'M NO WORSE THAN THE REST,"
YOU FAIL LIFE'S ULTIMATE TEST.

Praise be to the God and Father of our Lord Jesus Christ! In his great mercy he has given us new birth into a living hope through the resurrection of Jesus Christ from the dead, and into an inheritance that can never perish, spoil or fade—kept in heaven for you, who through faith are shielded by God's power until the coming of the salvation that is ready to be revealed in the last time. In this you greatly rejoice, though now for a little while you may have had to suffer grief in all kinds of trials. These have come so that your faith— of greater worth than gold, which perishes even though refined by fire—may be proved genuine and may result in praise, glory and honor when Jesus Christ is revealed. Though you have not seen him, you love him; and even though you do not see him now, you believe in him and are filled with an inexpressible and glorious joy, for you are receiving the goal of your faith, the salvation of your souls.

1 PETER 1:3-9

*B*ack in the 1970s, the personal world of Francis Schaeffer, Christian thinker and theologian, was invaded by cancer. When asked how his diagnosis affected him, Schaeffer said that his reaction, though not without tears, was similar to the reactions of his four children. All of them, in their own way, said, "Dad, I couldn't have taken it if you hadn't emphasized the Fall so completely in your teaching."

Schaeffer said that although most Christians strongly believe that the entrance of sin into the human race (Genesis 3) has had devastating effects on the world, many get angry or question God when disease or hardship invades the lives of believers.

When the apostle Peter wrote his first letter, he acknowledged that his readers had been visited by troubling circumstances (1:6). How did those early Christians react? Verse 6 tells us they rejoiced, for they cherished more than life itself the purifying effect of their trials—the proving and preserving of their faith.

One day, when we see Christ, much of our praise to Him will be the direct result of life's difficulties, which He has used for His wise purposes. But remember, our praise needn't wait until then!

~~~

GOD CAN USE LIFE'S SETBACKS TO MOVE US AHEAD.

What, after all, is Apollos? And what is Paul? Only servants, through whom you came to believe—as the Lord has assigned to each his task. I planted the seed, Apollos, watered it, but God made it grow. So neither he who plants nor he who waters is anything, but only God, who makes things grow. The man who plants and the man who waters have one purpose, and each will be rewarded according to his own labor. For we are God's fellow workers; you are God's field, God's building.

1 CORINTHIANS 3:5–9

While traveling in Finland, I appreciated the Finns' lavish use of candles. They never treat them as mere ornaments. Candles bring warmth and light into their homes during short winter days. The Finns know that a candle's purpose is missed unless it is burned. But candles should burn at one end only—a lesson I needed to learn.

When my husband and I began our missionary work, I longed to burn out for God. Within several years I had burned out all right, but not for God. Mine was a classic case of useless burnout, brought on by many self-caused stresses. I had forgotten that God had assigned me a task, and others had been assigned tasks as well. It was not all up to me.

One night I hit rock bottom and discovered that the rock was Christ. As He began teaching me dependence on Him for all things, the candle of my life was relighted for His use.

I now see a difference between so-called "Christian burnout" and "burning out for God." Burnout stems from wastefully burning the candle of our lives at both ends—hardly wise for candles or Christians. Burning out for God means our lives are spent wisely in His service—an echo of Paul's testimony in 2 Corinthians 12:15: "So I will very gladly spend for you everything I have and expend myself as well." Once used up for God, we'll be raised up for heavenly service (Revelation 22:3). It is for this purpose we were made!

~

WHAT'S IMPORTANT IS NOT HOW MUCH WE DO FOR GOD, BUT HOW MUCH GOD DOES THROUGH US.

Shout for joy, O heavens;
rejoice, O earth;
burst into song, O mountains!
For the LORD comforts his people
and will have compassion on his afflicted ones.
But Zion said, "The LORD has forsaken me,
the Lord has forgotten me."
"Can a mother forget the baby at her breast
and have no compassion on the child she has borne?
Though she may forget,
I will not forget you!
See, I have engraved you on the palms of my hands;
your walls are ever before me.

ISAIAH 49:13-16

Several mothers of small children were sharing encouraging answers to prayer. One woman admitted that she felt selfish when she troubled God with her personal needs. "Compared with the huge global needs God faces," she explained, "my circumstances must seem trivial to Him."

Moments later, her little son pinched his fingers in a door and ran screaming to his mother. She didn't say, "How selfish of you to bother me with your throbbing fingers when I'm busy!" No, she showed him great compassion and tenderness.

As Psalm 103:13 reminds us, this is the response of love, both human and divine. In Isaiah 49, God said that even though a mother may forget to have compassion on her child, the Lord never forgets! (v. 15). In picturesque language, God assured His people that He had inscribed them on the palms of His hands (v. 16).

Such intimacy with God belongs to those who fear Him and rely on Him rather than on themselves. As that child with throbbing fingers ran freely to his mother, so may we run to God with our daily problems.

The almighty God never has to neglect others to respond to your concerns. He has limitless time and love for each of His children. No need is too trivial for Him.

~~~

GOD BEARS THE WORLD'S WEIGHT ON HIS SHOULDER,
YET HOLDS HIS CHILDREN IN THE PALM OF HIS HAND.

CLEAN UP THE ENVIRONMENT

Therefore each of you must put off falsehood and speak truthfully to his neighbor, for we are all members of one body. "In your anger do not sin": Do not let the sun go down while you are still angry, and do not give the devil a foothold. He who has been stealing must steal no longer, but must work, doing something useful with his own hands, that he may have something to share with those in need.

Do not let any unwholesome talk come out of your mouths, but only what is helpful for building others up according to their needs, that it may benefit those who listen. And do not grieve the Holy Spirit of God, with whom you were sealed for the day of redemption. Get rid of all bitterness, rage and anger, brawling and slander, along with every form of malice. Be kind and compassionate to one another, forgiving each other, just as in Christ God forgave you.

EPHESIANS 4:25-32

*W*hat a frustrating problem pollution is! Everybody suffers from it, yet everybody contributes to it.

Pollution takes many forms, but one type is often overlooked. Charles Swindoll calls it "verbal pollution," passed around by grumblers, complainers, and criticizers. "The poison of pessimism," Swindoll writes, "creates an atmosphere of wholesale negativism where nothing but the bad side of everything is emphasized."

A group of Christian friends became concerned about this form of pollution and their personal part in it. So they made a pact to avoid critical words for a whole week. They were surprised to find how little they spoke! As they continued the experiment, they had to relearn conversation skills.

In Ephesians 4, Paul called believers to that sort of decisive action. He said we are to "put off" the old self and its conduct that grieves the Holy Spirit (v. 30) and "put on" the new self that builds up others (v. 24). As we rely on the help of the Spirit (Galatians 5:16), we can make those changes in our conduct, our thinking, and our speaking.

If we want to be rid of verbal pollution, we must choose to change and ask for God's help. It's a great way to start cleaning up our spiritual environment.

~~~

HELP STAMP OUT POLLUTION—CLEAN UP YOUR SPEECH!

So [Jesus] got up from the meal, took off his outer clothing, and wrapped a towel around his waist. After that, he poured water into a basin and began to wash his disciples' feet, drying them with the towel that was wrapped around him.

He came to Simon Peter, who said to him, "Lord, are you going to wash my feet?"

Jesus replied, "You do not realize now what I am doing, but later you will understand."

"No," said Peter, "you shall never wash my feet."

Jesus answered, "Unless I wash you, you have no part with me."

"Then, Lord," Simon Peter replied, "not just my feet but my hands and my head as well!"

Jesus answered, "A person who has had a bath needs only to wash his feet; his whole body is clean. And you are clean, though not every one of you." For he knew who was going to betray him, and that was why he said not every one was clean.

When he had finished washing their feet, he put on his clothes and returned to his place. "Do you understand what I have done for you?" he asked them. "You call me 'Teacher' and 'Lord,' and rightly so, for that is what I am. Now that I, your Lord and Teacher, have washed your feet, you also should wash one another's feet. I have set you an example that you should do as I have done for you."

JOHN 13:4–14

I once heard a preacher say, "The opposite of love is not hate—it's self!" That surprising statement reminded me of 2 Timothy 3:1–4, where Paul listed the signs of the end times. One of those signs is people who are "lovers of themselves" (v. 2). In sharp contrast to these self-saturated people are those whose lives are saturated with the servant attitude of Christ.

When Jesus washed the feet of His disciples, He gave us an example to follow. We too are to serve others selflessly.

That was the heart of what General William Booth, the founder of the Salvation Army, said just before he died. His little mission to the poor of London had spread across the world. His "soldiers" were gathered together at an international convention. General Booth had intended to be there to deliver the main address, but because he became ill he was unable to come. Those at the convention longed to receive a message from their beloved leader. So from his sickbed Booth dictated a one-word telegram that would be his last sermon. His final message was this: "Others!"

If we had to give our last word today, what would it be—a self word or a servant word? The time to decide is now, while we can still change.

~~~

JOY COMES BY PUTTING JESUS FIRST, OTHERS SECOND, AND YOURSELF LAST.

I thank Christ Jesus our Lord, who has given me strength, that he considered me faithful, appointing me to his service. Even though I was once a blasphemer and a persecutor and a violent man, I was shown mercy because I acted in ignorance and unbelief. The grace of our Lord was poured out on me abundantly, along with the faith and love that are in Christ Jesus.

Here is a trustworthy saying that deserves full acceptance: Christ Jesus came into the world to save sinners—of whom I am the worst. But for that very reason I was shown mercy so that in me, the worst of sinners, Christ Jesus might display his unlimited patience as an example for those who would believe on him and receive eternal life. Now to the King eternal, immortal, invisible, the only God, be honor and glory for ever and ever. Amen.

Timothy, my son, I give you this instruction in keeping with the prophecies once made about you, so that by following them you may fight the good fight, holding on to faith and a good conscience. Some have rejected these and so have shipwrecked their faith.

1 TIMOTHY 1:12–19

*M*y car has a wonderful feature. Whenever I forget to turn off the headlights, a shrill warning goes off the minute I open the door. I don't like its jarring sound, but I like what it saves me from—a dead battery.

Our conscience can work like that. When we sin or are tempted to, our conscience blows a whistle. It's a sign that the Holy Spirit is either convicting us of sin or warning us before we do. If we do wrong, the jarring feelings from our conscience are meant to lead us to repentance. When we confess and repent, God forgives and clears our conscience.

The apostle Paul knew what it was to have a bad conscience. In 1 Timothy 1:13, he wrote, "Even though I was once a blasphemer and a persecutor and a violent man, I was shown mercy because I acted in ignorance and unbelief." He received the mercy of Christ's forgiveness, faith, and a good conscience. He charged young Timothy to fight the good fight and maintain his faith and good conscience. Paul said that some had rejected these, and spiritual shipwreck was the result (vv. 18–19).

Be thankful if you have a good conscience. When it gives you a warning whistle, pay attention! Then fight to preserve your faith and keep your conscience clear. That jarring sound is there to help you stay in fellowship with Christ.

~

A GOOD CONSCIENCE IS ONE OF
THE BEST FRIENDS YOU'LL EVER HAVE.

NOTE TO THE READER

The publisher invites you to share your response to the message of this book by writing Discovery House Publishers, Box 3566, Grand Rapids, MI 49501, USA. For information about other Discovery House books, music, or videos, contact us at the same address or call 1-800-653-8333. Find us on the Internet at http://www.dhp.org/ or send e-mail to books@dhp.org.